Library of Shakespearean Biography and Criticism

I. PRIMARY REFERENCE WORKS ON SHAKESPEARE

II. CRITICISM AND INTERPRETATION

A. Textual Treatises, Commentaries
B. Treatment of Special Subjects
C. Dramatic and Literary Art in Shakespeare

III. SHAKESPEARE AND HIS TIME

A. General Treatises. Biography
B. The Age of Shakespeare
C. Authorship

Series II, Part A

The Sources of

MUCH ADO ABOUT NOTHING

Library of Shakespearean Biography and Criticism

The Sources of

MUCH ADO ABOUT NOTHING:

A Critical Study,
Together with the Text of Peter Beverley's
Ariodanto and Ieneura

By

Charles T. Prouty

 BOOKS FOR LIBRARIES PRESS

FREEPORT, NEW YORK

INTERNATIONAL STANDARD BOOK NUMBER:
0-8369-5513-7

LIBRARY OF CONGRESS CATALOG CARD NUMBER:
76-128893

PRINTED IN THE UNITED STATES OF AMERICA

To

A.H.R. Fairchild

PREFACE

SHAKESPEARE'S SOURCES have, since the time of Langbaine, been studied and commented upon. Not only in the Variorum but in separate volumes the materials which Shakespeare used have been reprinted and made available. Indicative of the general method of study are two such books as *Shakespeare's Plutarch* and *Shakespere's Holinshed* where are found those sections of the work of the two authors which underlie specific passages and scenes in the plays. But as Miss Campbell and Dr. Tillyard have demonstrated there is far more to be known about Shakespeare's borrowing from historical materials than is revealed by a study of those particular passages in Holinshed or Halle which it can be shown that he used. By the efforts of these scholars it is now generally realized that Shakespeare did not write his history plays in a sort of artistic isolation but that he followed consciously the Tudor *mythos* in his interpretation of history. Such studies have greatly illuminated one considerable aspect of the Elizabethan intellectual background.

The present study of *Much Ado About Nothing* is in a way related to such investigation of background material, but it approaches the problem through the actual sources with emphasis on the ideas found in them as compared with the ideas or concepts found in the play. Thus the focus is upon the structure, characters, and thematic unity of the play rather than on the background. The aim is to understand the raw materials as Shakespeare, the Elizabethan, probably understood them, with the possible result that we may thus come nearer to comprehending the purposes and processes of his creative intelligence. The final mystery of genius will always elude us; but I hope that this method of investigation—one which I plan to apply in somewhat more general terms to the three Joyous Comedies as a group—may enhance, in some small measure, our critical and aesthetic perception.

The only one of the major sources of the play which is not available in the Variorum or in reprint form is Peter Beverley's *The Historie of Ariodanto and Ieneura* which is extant in a uniqe copy at the Henry E. Huntington Library and Art Gallery of San Marino, California. The reprinting of this poem which constitutes a part of the present volume has seemed desirable so that all the principal source materials might be available. In its own right, Beverley's poem is worthy of notice since it is the first English adaptation of even a part of the *Orlando Furioso*. Secondly, as an exemplar of the early Elizabethan interest in translation from French and Italian narratives it antedates Painter and Fenton. The recent work of M. Pruvost on Belleforest and that of Mr. Frank Hook on Fenton's translations have made clear the value of studying this movement for its influence on later Elizabethan fiction, romance, and drama.

I am indebted to the Henry E. Huntington Library for permission to reprint the text of Beverley.

My colleagues and friends have been generous in reading the manuscript and advising me, so I wish to record my gratitude to Professors Albert Feuillerat, Helge Kökeritz, R. J. Menner, S. B. Hemingway, and E. T. Donaldson of Yale, as well as to Doctors James G. McManaway and Giles E. Dawson of the Folger Shakespeare Library and finally to Mr. David Horne who has examined for me documents in the British Museum and Somerset House.

New Haven, Conn.   C. T. P.
February, 1950.

CONTENTS

I

THE PROBLEM

In practically any modern edition of *Much Ado About Nothing,* a reader will find a section devoted to the sources of the play. Here he will learn that Shakespeare borrowed his main plot from Bandello or Belleforest, and the trick of deception from Spenser or Ariosto; but that Dogberry, Verges, the Watch, and Benedick and Beatrice are Shakespeare's original creations. Since these facts are well known it would seem that there is little to be learned from any further study of sources. There are, however, two principal critical problems, as well as several minor ones, which may be clarified by a fresh examination of the source materials and their relation to the finished play.

The first of these is the connection between the two plots, one borrowed and one invented. There is general critical agreement that the main plot is noncomic and that the humor of the play is found in Shakespeare's original characters. While this statement is obviously true, it is, after all, merely descriptive and exhibits no curiosity as to Shakespeare's reasons for adding these particular new creations to this particular old story. It is my belief that these reasons are not beyond conjecture, although hitherto no one seems to have been concerned with them. Instead critics and editors alike echo the opinion expressed by Miss Mary Augusta Scott.

Having decided upon his plot, meaning it for a main plot, I fancy the poet casting about for something bright to enliven it.[1]

In 1938 Professor Parrott said much the same sort of thing:

They [Benedick and Beatrice] are Shakespeare's creations added by him to put the salt of life into the borrowed unreal and sentimental plot.[2]

More recently the same critic observed,

The main plot, one, as we have seen, of peculiar interest to his age, Shakespeare has handled in such a way as to make it little more than a background for a theme of his own invention, a battle of the sexes between two such lively duelists as Benedick and Beatrice.[3]

In other words it would seem that the main plot serves only as a frame-

1. *"The Book of the Courtyer:* A Possible Source for Benedick and Beatrice," *PMLA,* XVI (1901), 490.
2. Thomas Marc Parrott, *Shakespeare Twenty-Three Plays and the Sonnets* (New York, 1938), p. 480.
3. Thomas Marc Parrott, *Shakespearean Comedy* (New York, 1949), p. 162.

work for the display of Benedick and Beatrice as well as Dogberry and his compeers. While it is nowhere stated, the conclusion appears to be that there is no thematic or structural unity in the play. The best that can be said is that the characters of one plot appear in the other. Such a view is enforced by the theory of revision which the New Cambridge editors [4] put forward in 1923 and which has gained wide acceptance. In 1598, according to them, the dramatist revised an old play in which he had portrayed the story of Hero and Claudio. Revising, Shakespeare expanded the parts of Benedick and Beatrice, letting "them take charge of the audience, relegating Don John and Claudio—even Hero herself and the whole stage-plot into the background of our interest." The question of *why* Benedick and Beatrice were introduced into the old play is not discussed by these editors, nor by subsequent editors, except in the usual terms of comic interpolation. Typical is the comment of Professor Charlton on Beatrice:

. . . we take her to have been grafted by Shakespeare on to an earlier play of his own which thus became *Much Ado* . . .[5]

That there might be any reason for the grafting of Beatrice on to this particular old story is neither suggested nor discussed. Professor Harrison admits the possibility of revision and with it, certainly by implication, the theory of capricious combination.[6] Professor Craig goes a bit beyond the original revision theory:

. . . Shakespeare, having made a great hit on the stage with the merry war of courtship between a resolved old bachelor [aged Benedick?] and a woman who was a man-hater, modified the play, probably while it was on the stage, by fattening these parts and, in order to find room for the new matter, which is written in prose, abridged the major plot which had been written mainly in verse . . .[7]

It is most certainly true that Shakespeare was a working dramatist, but it may not be amiss to suggest that this view of him has obscured the fact that he was also a dramatic artist. The comments which have been cited seem to imply that his handling of his plot materials was at best capricious and was designed primarily to appeal to the vagaries of popular taste. Such, indeed, was the tenor of Coleridge's criticism of Dogberry, Verges, and the Watch; for he observed, ". . . any other less ingenuously absurd watchmen and night-constables would have an-

---

4. *Much Ado About Nothing*, ed. Sir Arthur Quiller-Couch and John Dover Wilson (Cambridge, 1923), introd., p. ix. The evidence for revision is discussed by Professor Wilson on pp. 92–102. Miss Grace Trenery, the editor of the Arden Edition ([London, 1924], pp. xvi–xxi), discussed the theory and its "slender foundations."
5. H. B. Charlton, *Shakespearian Comedy* (London, 1938), p. 284.
6. G. B. Harrison, *Shakespeare 23 Plays and the Sonnets* (New York, 1948), p. 418.
7. Hardin Craig, *An Interpretation of Shakespeare* (New York, 1948), p. 121.

swered the necessities of the action." The implications of this remark led Dr. Furness [8] to make vigorous objection.

An idea is thereby conveyed that SHAKESPEARE worked, to a certain extent, at hap-hazard, or, at least, that at times he lost sight of the requirements of his story and was willing to vary the characters of his creation at the suggestion of caprice, to introduce a blundering constable here or a drunken porter there just to lighten his play or to raise a horse-laugh in the groundlings. It would be difficult to imagine a falser imputation on SHAKE-SPEARE'S consummate art. Never did SHAKESPEARE lose sight of the trending of his story; not a scene, I had almost said not a phrase, did he write that does not reveal the true hard-working artist labouring, with undeviating gaze, to produce a certain effect.

Dr. Furness agreed that Dogberry and the Watch do "supply endless mirth," but he also showed that these are the exact characters needed for Shakespeare's particular purpose. The humor is not extraneous; it is a carefully planned part of the dramatic structure. Similarly, it is my belief that Benedick and Beatrice are an integral part of the play and are not solely introduced for comic relief. In other words, the joining of the two plots, one borrowed and one original, was purposeful, not capricious, for although we most certainly enjoy ourselves when we read or see *Much Ado,* it will be found that here, as elsewhere, Shakespeare is expressing his reaction to a certain aspect of life. This expression, or the idea of which the play is the expression, dictated the form and development of the play. Having read Bandello or Belleforest and being familiar with the ideas and points of view implicit in these and other retellings of the familiar story, Shakespeare conceived an idea for a play, and his reaction to the traditional story was peculiarly his own, as we shall observe.

The second critical problem is that of the nature of the main plot. Professor Parrott, as we have noted, calls it "unreal and sentimental." Mark Van Doren [9] refers to "the tragedy of Claudio and Hero," while Professor Spencer [10] says, "The main plot, the wooing of Hero, is highly romantic." Professor Harrison [11] describes it as "weak, melodramatic and to modern readers almost offensive, because after his outrageous conduct, Claudio's undeserved reward affronts the sense of justice." The "outrageous conduct of Claudio" provoked nineteenth-century critics to cries of indignation and anger. As Professor Kittredge [12] notes, Swinburne calls him "a pitiful fellow" and Andrew Lang is equally harsh: "he

---

8. *Much Ado About Nothing,* ed. H. H. Furness (Variorum Edition, Philadelphia, 1900), p. xxxii.

9. Mark Van Doren, *Shakespeare* (New York, 1939), p. 141.

10. Hazelton Spencer, *The Art and Life of William Shakespeare* (New York, 1940), p. 241.

11. *Op. cit.,* p. 418.

12. *Much Ado About Nothing,* ed. G. L. Kittredge (Boston, 1941), p. xii.

behaves throughout like the most hateful young cub." More recently we find such references as "the shameful conduct of Claudio"; [13] "Claudio's ready belief in the accusation springs from his own suspicious temper." [14] On the other hand Claudio has been excused and defended. Some critics [15] point out that "seeing is believing," and Professor Spencer [16] observes, "A good actor can make Claudio's youth, grief, and bewilderment sympathetic." Elsewhere we read of "the romantic Claudio," [17] "the vain young sentimentalist"; [18] find him compared to Orlando and Romeo,[19] and see him, through one critic,[20] "as a kind of romantic Orlando brought face to face with dismal fact."

This wide divergence of opinions as to the nature of the main plot and the character of Claudio poses a problem; but I believe that a resolution of it may be found in a comparison of the source materials and the finished play. The main plot and Claudio need to be understood in Elizabethan terms, but these have been obscured by time and, in some cases, by subjective judgments as well. Here Shakespeare's alterations of and additions to his borrowed materials will assist us in reaching an understanding. By inquiring why additions and alterations were made, we may see Claudio as Shakespeare and an Elizabethan audience saw him, and similarly we can realize the significance of the main plot and its relation to the organic structure and thematic unity of the play as a whole. As far as I know, there has been no attempt to view the play in this fashion, and I would suggest that the failure to do so has been the chief reason for the easy acceptance of Benedick and Beatrice as capricious comic interpolation and for the divergence of judgments on the significance of the main plot and the character of Claudio. Since on the one hand we have the raw material and on the other, the finished product, it is possible to understand, to some extent, the sea change which took place in Shakespeare's mind.

But to reach any such understanding we must share, at least in part, the view expressed by Dr. Furness that Shakespeare was a conscious artist who knew what he was doing, who wanted to please his audience but did so by making the scenes and characters of comedy an integral, not an extraneous, part of his play. To perceive the play as a whole it will be necessary to put aside the impression that in *Much Ado* we have a haphazard combination of elements related only because the characters of one plot appear in the events of the other. Theoretically the idea and

13. E. E. Stoll, *Shakespeare Studies* (New York, 1929), p. 72.
14. Parrott, *Shakespearean Comedy*, p. 162.
15. Craig, *op. cit.*, p. 120; Kittredge, *op. cit.*
16. *Op. cit.*, p. 255.
17. E. E. Stoll, *Shakespeare and Other Masters* (Cambridge, Massachusetts, 1940), p. 36.
18. Trenery, *op. cit.*, p. xix.
19. Stoll, *Shakespeare Studies*, p. 74.
20. D. L. Stevenson, *The Love-Game Comedy* (New York, 1946), pp. 208–209.

the unity of the play should be apparent to a spectator or reader who is familiar with the Elizabethan scene, but the frequent disparagement of the main plot suggests a possible reason why the play has not been completely understood.

For some reason or other the plot which is now so little esteemed was immensely popular in the Renaissance. At present we know of some eighteen versions of the tale written during the sixteenth century prior to Shakespeare's play. Even though we may not share this earlier liking for the story, we shall not understand *Much Ado* unless we have some idea of the reasons for such popularity. In this connection Peter Beverley's *Ariodanto and Ieneura* (1565–66) [21] is of considerable value, for in this first English appearance of the story we shall find much that is significant, and for this reason it has seemed worth while to reprint, for the first time, the text of the poem. But in addition to studying new material it will be useful to know why, with the exceptions of the translations of Ariosto by Harington, Taillemont, and Saint Gelais and De Baïf, no two versions are alike. Source study in this instance will be concerned, therefore, not so much with the borrowing of particular details, names, and setting as with the ideological provenance of the story. What this narrative meant to a variety of representative sixteenth-century poets, dramatists, and *novellieri* will indicate its significance to Shakespeare and his audience.

The development of this particular story is not unusual; many another tale was variously treated by different authors, and this is what we should expect of Renaissance authors familiar with the critical precepts of their age. In particular the doctrine of imitation, understood in the light of Renaissance opinion, makes it abundantly clear that variety rather than similarity is to be expected in the retelling of a popular narrative.

This doctrine is clearly expressed in the literature and critical works of the period, and its origins and prevalence have been the subject of a valuable study by Dr. Harold White. [22] In spite of, or perhaps because of, the currency of the concept, it is rarely mentioned in connection with any study of sources, either dramatic or nondramatic. Although introductions to Shakespeare's plays invariably notice the sources of individual plays, presumably the reader, layman, or scholar accepts the fact without questioning "Why?" or "How?" Shakespeare utilized the work of other men. As a matter of fact Shakespeare was following the prevailing tendency of his age in borrowing plot materials. To state the fact thus simply does not explain or even suggest its possible implications. To realize as nearly as we can why Shakespeare borrowed and how he handled such materials may clarify themes and ideas which have been obscured by

21. For full title see below, p. 72.
22. *Plagiarism and Imitation During the English Renaissance* (Cambridge, Massachusetts, 1935).

time and by personal judgments based on nineteenth- or twentieth-century standards. Practically all Renaissance works of fiction, both dramatic and nondramatic, have sources even as do Shakespeare's plays, and both authors and critics of the time discuss the general doctrine of imitation which underlies this reuse of old materials in the creation of new works. Since the doctrine is a beginning point in source study, it may not be amiss to review the facts of the matter, even though to some they will be well known.

The various critical treatises of the Renaissance discuss imitation from many points of view: some deal with the improvement of style which will result from a careful imitation of the manner of Cicero; others advocate imitation of both the manner and matter of the ancients. In all such discussions, however, a recurrent theme is the necessity for telling the truth in order to evade the Platonic charge that poets are liars. Imitation of matter is essential unless the writer is to be guilty of the most serious charge of fabrication and invention. Very simply, both theory and practice in the Renaissance held that a plot should be based on historical fact or on that which custom and tradition had dignified as being the equivalent of historical fact or anything which the author might have known to have happened either at first hand or by report. The appearance of the word *Historie* in the title of Beverley's narrative, for example, is supposed to imply that this obligation has been fufilled. Thus we may understand why the novellieri usually introduce their tales within a specific setting and with explicit guarantees that what they are about to relate actually had taken place. Masuccio di Salerno in the "Parlamento de l'auttore al Libro suo" to *Le cinqvanta novelle* says: ". . . invoca l'altissimo Dio per testimonio che tutte son verisimile historie, e le piú negli nostri moderni tempi avenute . . ." [23] One of these contemporary histories which the author calls upon God to witness as being like unto the truth is the story of Mariotto and Giannozza of Siena, which is best known to the modern reader in Shakespeare's version, *Romeo and Juliet*. Some fifty-odd years after Masuccio, Luigi da Porto told the story but changed the scene from Siena to Verona and the names of the lovers to Romeo and Giuletta. Da Porto was so convinced of the truth of his tale that he dated the sad events as occurring in the years 1301–04 and claimed to have heard the story from a Veronese guard. By 1831 the fiction, which had its ultimate origin in the *Ephesiaca* of Xenophon, was described as true history by an Italian scholar,[24] and the guides of Verona led visitors to the tomb of their city's most famous lovers.

English authors were equally concerned with the veracity of their

23. Masuccio Salernitano, *Le cinqvanta novelle* [Stessa, Venice, ca. 1535], fol. 207ᵛ.
24. *La pietosa morte di Giulia Cappelletti e Romeo Montecchi, lettere critiche di Filippo Scolari*, ed. Alessandro Torri (Livorno, 1831). The three letters maintain the historical truth of the story. Torri concurs.

writings. Richard Edwards emphasized this in the prologue to his tragi-comedy, *Damon and Pithias:*

> It is no legend-lie
> But a thing once done, indeed, as histories do descry.[25]

The folly of dealing with anything but the truth is made clear in the opening lines of Gascoigne's verse narrative, "Dan Bartholmew of Bathe."

> To tell a tale without authoritye,
> Or fayne a Fable by invention,
> That one proceedes of quicke capacitye,
> That other proves but small discretion . . .[26]

Spenser, well aware of the sins of invention and fabrication, anticipates objections to his work on such grounds in the first stanza of the second book of *The Faerie Queene.*

> Right well I wote most mighty Soueraine,
> That all this famous antique history,
> Of some th'aboundance of an idle braine
> Will judged be, and painted forgery,
> Rather then matter of iust memory,
> Sith none, that breatheth liuing aire, does know,
> Where is that happy land of Faery,
> Which I so much do vaunt, yet no where show,
> But vouch antiquities, which no body can know.[27]

But "Faery land" is not a forgery; it is real and true, or as the poet tells Elizabeth:

> And thou, O fairest Princesse vnder sky,
> In this faire mirrhour maist behold thy face,
> And thine owne realmes in lond of Faery,
> And in this antique Image thy great auncestry.[28]

His truth is his own observation of the world in which he lived. That world was also Shakespeare's, and we shall see, a bit later, that on one occasion both poets observed the same phenomena and both had similar reactions to what they saw.

25. *Chief Pre-Shakespearean Dramas,* ed. J. Q. Adams (Boston, 1924), p. 572, ll. 31–32.

At least one Elizabethan reader was equally concerned with such differentiation as we may observe on the title page of one copy of Greene's *The Scottish Historie of James the fourth* (ed. Collins, II, 87) where the words following "Historie" have been lined through and above them has been written "or rather fiction of English and Scotish matters comicall."

26. *George Gascoigne's A Hundreth Sundrie Flowres,* ed. C. T. Prouty, *University of Missouri Studies,* XVII, No. 2 (Columbia, 1942), 195.

27. *The Poetical Works of Edmund Spenser,* ed. J. C. Smith and E. de Selincourt (London, 1926), p. 69.

28. *Ibid.*

Due observation of truth did not mean that the creative artist was merely an historiographer whose office was "to tell things as they were done without either augmenting and diminishing them, or swaruing one iote from the truth." [29] The poet did have the right to augment, diminish, and "swarue," or as Spenser observes in the letter to Raleigh: *"For the Methode of a Poet historical is not such, as of an Historiographer. For an Historiographer discourseth of affayres orderly as they were donne, accounting as well the times as the actions, but a Poet thrusteth into the middest, euen where it most concerneth him . . ."* [30] The concern of the poet, either "historical" or nonhistorical, was to develop and interpret his raw material. This problem is, like nearly all aspects of cultural life of the Renaissance, discussed in *The Book of the Courtier.* Sir Frederick inquiring whether the ancients did not imitate is answered by Count Lewis who emphasizes the necessity for reinterpretation or "wading further." "An if Virgill had altogether folowed Hesiodus, he should not have passed him nor Cicero, Crassus, nor Ennius, his predecessors. . . . And truly it should be a great miserye to stoppe without wading any farther then almost the first that ever wrote . . ." [31]

Here the concern of the poet is described in general terms, but critical writings of the period and the examples of what authors did in practice indicate that originality was exercised in two consonant developments. The Renaissance author reinterpreted his source in terms of his own individual reaction to the events or ideas which it contained. This reinterpretation might also be termed improvement or "polishing," but this term has a somewhat specialized meaning: it applies usually to rhetorical elaboration and adornment rather than to a revaluation of the ideas implicit in a source. This latter process results from an author's being a man of his times possessed of the various ideological, spiritual, and intellectual stereotypes of that time. Thus his view of his source is modified, and thus he reinterprets. In the course of reinterpretation he will most naturally improve by rhetorical elaboration and adornment. These aspects of source study are those which have been neglected, for hitherto most research on the subject has been concerned with specific borrowings of names of characters and places, details of plot, and parallel passages. Important and valuable though such factual observations are, they are after all but the beginning.

In the task at hand it is necessary to know not only the plots of the many versions of the story and the details which are common to each of them and to Shakespeare; we must know as well why the various authors handled the basic plot situation as they did. Only by careful study and by

29. Thomas Blundeville, *The True Order and Methode of Wryting and Reading Hystories* (London, 1574), sig. E4ᵛ. Folger Shakespeare Library copy.

30. *The Poetical Works of Edmund Spenser*, p. 408.

31. Baldassare Castiglione, *The Book of the Courtier*, trans. Sir Thomas Hoby, 1561, ed. Walter Raleigh (London, 1900), pp. 74, 76.

understanding as best we can the intellectual atmosphere of the time may we estimate such tenuous ideas as an author's reason or purpose in the treatment of his raw materials. Perhaps the value and importance in such a study of a variety of second- and third-rate material may be clarified by reference to Shakespeare and his handling of sources in such a play as *As You Like It.* The facts are easily ascertained: the source is Lodge's *Rosalynde,* and Shakespeare follows this romance quite closely. He does, however, omit nearly a third of the story, specifically that part which deals with the brotherly strife between Rosader (Orlando) and his elder brother Saladyne (Oliver). Such cutting may be easily explained on the simple ground that Shakespeare is interested in this quarrel only insofar as it serves his purpose in getting Orlando banished and on his way to the forest of Arden. This is all very well, but a question still remains. Why does he follow the rest of the romance so closely? Why, to turn to another play, does he follow Arthur Brooke's poem so faithfully in *Romeo and Juliet?* Why, on the other hand, are there no such easy and closely related sources for *Much Ado* and *Twelfth Night?* The explanation of such questions is not readily found; but it would seem that an attempt to answer them might not be without value, for the search would lead us to an inquiry into Shakespeare's attitude toward his sources and the ideas which motivated his reinterpretation.

In such an inquiry we must first comprehend Shakespeare's raw materials: it is not enough to read Lodge's *Rosalynde* or the manifold versions of the *Much Ado* story; we must be reasonably certain that we understand these sources in relation to their own intellectual and literary milieu. The development of the basic plot of *Much Ado* from the simple narratives of Ariosto and Bandello to the elaborate and sophisticated versions of such men as Beverley and Whetstone suggests not merely reinterpretation but reinterpretation which is allied to a general progression and alteration of ideas and literary tastes. Seen as a part of the pattern of the age, the successive treatments of the tale are more readily comprehensible to us, and we are then able to view the basic plot materials in something of the same fashion as did Shakespeare. Whether we believe that Shakespeare was a faithful epitome of that amorphous figure, "the Elizabethan man," or whether we hold that Shakespeare was specifically individualistic, reflecting a variety of attitudes, some medieval, some Renaissance, and some surprisingly modern, the fact remains that he did live and have his being in an England ruled by Elizabeth and James. Because we have no record of discussions between Shakespeare and his contemporaries on the general topic of man's behavior, emotions, thoughts, and ideals, it is not necessary to deny to him any such conversations or reflections. Nor should we isolate him from the currents of the Renaissance because he was a man of genius who perceived and recorded certain essentials of human experience. If the observation of men's hopes and fears, their moments of greatness and of weakness which we so esteem in his plays be a fair guide, Shakespeare had a capacious intelligence and a keen comprehension of the world in which he lived. Whether he approved or disapproved, he was aware of the patterns and thoughts of his age, and it is no unwarranted assumption to say that such a man understood perfectly well the changing concepts of love behavior which affected the development of the materials he employed in *Much Ado*.

The foregoing is not meant to imply that Shakespeare sat down to write with some ten or a dozen of the sources before him, although I have no doubt that he read both Italian and French and was familiar with both Bandello and Belleforest. But to know as nearly as we can the significance of the story to Shakespeare, the Elizabethan, we must be aware of the changing and developing attitudes as to the proper behavior of lovers which affected each of the many authors and, finally, Shakespeare. As has been said the alterations, omissions, and additions will thus take on new importance as indications of the playwright's method and purpose. Whether or no the text of *Much Ado* is a revision is not germane to this study, since the play as it stands shows the results of purposeful construction, not capricious interpolation. Shakespeare was a man of the theater, but he was not a hack or a patcher of old clouts; he was a skilled playwright who had definite reactions to life and experience and who was, as Miss Campbell [32] has recently called to our attention, singularly purposeful in the construction of plot. It is with a view to realizing this purpose in *Much Ado About Nothing* that a new study of the sources seems worth while.

32. Lily B. Campbell, "Shakespeare and Shaw: Plot or Preface," a paper read before the Modern Language Association, December 28, 1948.

II

THE SOURCES

The first notice of the sources of *Much Ado About Nothing* is found in Gerard Langbaine's *Account of the English Dramatick Poets* (1691). In his account of Shakespeare Langbaine sought to indicate, insofar as he was able, the sources of a variety of plays including many that were apocryphal. Although his knowledge was far from complete, he does seem to have been familiar with a fair amount of English and continental literature. Cinthio is mentioned in connection with *Measure for Measure* and *Othello;* Bandello, with *Romeo and Juliet;* and Boccaccio, with *All's Well* and *Cymbeline.* Plautus, Plutarch, and the English historians all are noted. Although Greene's *Pandosto* is cited for *The Winter's Tale,* Lodge's *Rosalynde* is not mentioned nor is any source given for *As You Like It.* Of *Much Ado* he observes: ". . . the contrivance of *Borachio,* in behalf of *John* the Bastard to make *Claudio* jealous of *Hero,* by the Assistance of her Waiting-Woman *Margaret,* is borrowed from *Ariosto's Orlando Furioso:* see Book the fifth in the Story of *Lurcanio,* and *Geneuza* [*sic*]: the like Story is in *Spencer's Fairy Queen,* Book 2. Canto 4." [1]

To each book of his translation of the *Orlando Furioso* Sir John Harington appended a commentary which dealt with such topics as: "Morall," "Storie," "Allegorie," and "Allusion." Under this last heading in the commentary on the fifth book we find the following:

Allusion there is in this tale of Geneura, *vnto a storie written in* Alciats duello, *of a matron in* Fraunce *accused in such sort, by two men, and a certain souldier of Barcellona came with a companion of his, and tooke vpon them the defence of the woman, and being fighting, the companion of the souldier fled: notwithstanding he of Barcellona with his courage and vertue gat the victorie of the other two, and so in strange attire went home to his countrey vnknowne, to which* Ariodant *seems to allude. Some others affirme, that this very matter, though set downe here by other names, happened in Ferrara to a kinsewoman of the Dukes, which is here figured vnder the name of* Geneura, *and that in deede such a practise was vsed against her by a great Lord, & discouered by a dāsel as is here set downe. Howsoeuer it was, sure the tale is a pretie comicall matter, & hath bin writtē in English verse some few years past (learnedly & with good grace) though in verse of another kind, by* M. George Turberuil.[2]

---

1. Gerard Langbaine, *An Account of the English Dramatick Poets* (Oxford, 1691), pp. 460–461. The story is found in Cantos IV, V, and VI of the *Orlando Furioso,* and in Bk. II, Canto 4, sts. 3–33 of *The Faerie Queene.*

2. *Orlando Furioso in English Heroical Verse* (London, 1607), p. 39. The first edition

Since no such poem by Turbervile survives and since there is no record of any, it is likely that Harington's memory played him false and that the poem referred to was Peter Beverley's *Historie of Ariodanto and Ieneura.* Perhaps Harington was thinking of this as being included in Turbervile's *Tragical Tales,* although if he was, it is none too easy to explain the descriptive phrase, "a pretie comicall matter."

In the eighteenth century Thomas Warton knew Beverley's poem and noted it as "a paraphrase in verse" of a story from Ariosto.[3] He did not, however, connect it with *Much Ado,* and until recent times this narrative has been thought lost. The literary past and particularly Shakespeare interested a number of Warton's contemporaries. In 1753 Mrs. Charlotte Lennox published the first collection of Shakespearean sources under the title, *Shakespear Illustrated.*[4] This contained a prose translation of the relevant material from Ariosto but no new material for *Much Ado.* Edward Capell, however, made a noteworthy contribution to the sources of this play when he called attention to Bandello's twentieth *novella* and Belleforest's translation thereof, "Histoire Disuitiesme." [5]

Early in the next century John Dunlop published *The History of Fiction* which contained a wealth of information about Shakespeare's sources and the interrelations of different versions of them. Practically all of Dunlop's references have been incorporated in later work, but his contribution should be better recognized than it is. In discussing *Tirante el blanco,* Johan Martorell's romance written about 1400, Dunlop calls attention to "a stratagem resembling that which deceives Claudio in Much Ado About Nothing, and also the lover of Geneura in the fifth canto of the Orlando Furioso." [6]

The research of other nineteenth-century scholars, as well as that of their predecessors, was summarized by Furness in the Variorum edition

appeared in 1591. In the *Dvello de lo Eccellentissimo, e Clarissimo Giurisconsulto M. Andrea Alciato* ([Venice, 1544], fol. 13r) the story is as Harington tells it; nothing is said as to why or how the matron was accused.

3. Thomas Warton, *History of English Poetry,* ed. W. Carew Hazlitt (London, 1871), IV, 350. Warton (p. 341) also notices Bishop Tanner's mention of "a prose English version of the *Novelle* of Bandello, wh[ich] endeavoured to avoid the obscenities of Boccaccio and the improbabilities of Cinthio: in 1580 by W.W." No trace of any such translation survives aside from its notice by Bishop Tanner. It is this lost translation which Professor Allison Gaw ("Is Shakespeare's *Much Ado* a Revised Earlier Play?" *PMLA,* L [1935], 722) would have to be Shakespeare's source for the Bandello-Belleforest elements.

4. (London, 1753–54), III, 231–256.

5. *Mr. William Shakespeare his Comedies, Histories and Tragedies,* ed. Edward Capell (10 vols., London, 1768), I, 65. Capell also mentions Spenser and Harington. The Italian is found in *La Prima Parte De Le Novelle Del Bandello* (Lucca, 1554), fols. 149r–166r; the French in Belleforest's *Le Troisième Tome Des Histoires Tragiques extraittes des oeuvres Italiennes de Bandel* (Lyon, 1574), fols. 473v–514v. I have used the Folger Shakespeare Library copies of Bandello and Belleforest.

6. John Dunlop, *The History of Fiction* (London, 1845), p. 169.

THE SOURCES

of *Much Ado* (1899). The relevant sections of the *Orlando* and *The Faerie Queene* and a full translation of Bandello's novella were here reprinted. Printed in abstract were Belleforest's translation of Bandello and Jacob Ayrer's *Die schoene Phaenecia,* a dramatic adaptation of the Bandello story written sometime between 1593 and 1605. A synopsis of Starter's Dutch adaptation of Bandello entitled, *Blyeyndich-Truyrspel, van Timbre de Cardone ende Fenicie van Messine* (1618), and a digest of Duke Heinrich Julius' *Vincentius Ladiszlous,* a German play printed in 1599 which served as a source for some of Baron Munchausen's better adventures but in which Herman Grimm fancied he saw the origin of Benedick, round out the collection of sources. Notice is given Weichberger's attempt to find some connection between the Greek romance *Chaereas and Callirhoe* of Chariton and the novels of Bandello and Cinthio.[7]

With M. Feuillerat's publication of the Revels' Accounts notice of two lost plays testified further to the popularity of the story. Richard Mulcaster, headmaster of the Merchant Taylors' School, took his boys to court on February 12, 1583, for a performance of *Ariodante and Geneura.*[8] My guess would be that this was possibly a dramatization of Beverley's poem. The other play is more doubtful. On January 1, 1575, Leicester's company presented at court "the matter of Panecia."[9] The name may well be a corruption of "Fenecia" and if such be the case, the play was adapted from Bandello.

In 1931 a full account of the background and development of Ariosto's story of Genevra was included in Dr. Barbara Matulka's *The Novels of Juan de Flores and Their European Diffusion.*[10] From De Flores' *Grisel y Mirabella* Ariosto borrowed the "cruel law of Scotland" theme. This was the law which condemned to the stake a woman charged with fornication unless her innocence were upheld by a champion appearing in her behalf. While this theme is an integral part of Ariosto's tale, it does not appear in Bandello or in Shakespeare and so is of no great concern to us. Of interest is Dr. Matulka's list of English, French, and Italian appearances of the Genevra episode. Although most of these have been noted elsewhere or appeared subsequent to Shakespeare's play, two references

7. The sources are discussed on pp. 295–347. Cinthio's version tells of the servant Gianetta who disguises herself as her mistress and with an accomplice convinces the concealed husband of his wife's unfaithfulness. Since Gianetta is a jealous woman who seeks to advance her own cause, the story is obviously an imitation of *Tirante el blanco.* It is found in *Hecatommithi overo Cento Novelle di M. Giovanbattista Giraldi Cinthio* (Venice, 1574), fol. 45ᵛ. Folger Shakespeare Library copy.
8. *Documents Relating to the Office of the Revels in the Time of Queen Elizabeth,* ed. A. Feuillerat, *Materialien zur Kunde des älteren Englischen Dramas,* Bd. XXI (Louvain, 1908), p. 350.
9. *Ibid.,* p. 238.
10. "Comparative Literature Series" (The Institute of French Studies, New York, 1931).

are new. In 1556 Claude de Taillemont published *La Tricarite* which contained a prose imitation of Ariosto entitled, "Le conte de l'infante Genevre figle du Roy d'Escosse pris du Furieux et fet Françoes." [11] A few years later, on February 13, 1564, members of the court presented at Fontainebleau a play on the same subject.[12] The latter is unfortunately lost, but presumably it would have been something like Mulcaster's play.

An English play which has survived and which is of possible interest in this discussion is *Two Italian Gentlemen* (1585),[13] a translation, or rather adaptation, of Luigi Pasqualigo's *Il Fedele*.[14] F. C. Danchin has pointed out that the deception is similar to that found in *Much Ado*.[15] In reality the connection is tenuous, but the play is worth noting together with Abraham Fraunce's Latin comedy *Victoria*,[16] also a translation of *Il Fedele*.

In 1941 I called attention to Beverley and Whetstone,[17] and a year later D. J. Gordon discussed Della Porta's *Gli duoi fratelli rivali* as a possible source.[18] If to all the foregoing we add the translation of the Genevra episode from Ariosto begun by Saint Gelais and finished by De Baïf,[19] the list of all sixteenth-century versions which are now known is complete.[20]

11. *Ibid.*, p. 194. Dr. Matulka relies on Th. Roth's *Der Einfluss von Ariost's Orlando Furioso auf das Französische Theater* (Leipzig, 1905), pp. 205–206, where there is a brief mention of the story. Roth wonders whether Taillemont's work was derived from a play such as that presented at Fontainebleau or whether the play was based on Taillemont. Evidently Roth had not seen *La Tricarite*, for he refers to Du Verdier's *La Bibliothèque* as his authority. *La Tricarite* is a very scarce work which has never been reprinted and I have been unable to examine a copy.

12. Matulka, *op. cit.*, p. 194. The earliest modern notice of this was by Jacques Madeleine in "La Belle Genièvre, première en date des tragi-comédies françaises," *Revue de la Renaissance*, IV (1903), 30–46.

13. M.[unday] A.[nthony], *Fedele and Fortvnio. The deceites in Loue: excellently discoursed in a very pleasant and fine conceited Comoedie, of two Italian Gentlemen* (London, 1585). The one perfect copy of this play is in the Folger Shakespeare Library. The play was edited for the Malone Society by Percy Simpson in 1909.

14. *Il Fedele Comedia Del Clarissimo M. Lvigi Pasqvaligo* (Venice, 1579).

15. "Une source de *Much Ado About Nothing, Revue anglo-américaine*, XIII (1937), 430–431.

16. *Victoria, a Latin Comedy by Abraham Fraunce*, ed. G. C. Moore Smith (Louvain, 1906) (*Materialien*, Bd. XIV).

17. "George Whetstone, Peter Beverly, and the Sources of *Much Ado About Nothing*," *Studies in Philology*, XXXVIII (1941), 211–220. "The Discourse of Rinaldo and Giletta" occupies pp. 23–45 in the first section of *The Rocke of Regard* (London, 1576). Each of the four parts of this work is paginated separately. In J. P. Collier's reprint of *The Rocke of Regard* (London, 1866–70) it occupies pp. 41–90.

18. "*Much Ado About Nothing:* A Possible Source for the Hero-Claudio Plot," *Studies in Philology*, XXXIX (1942), 279–290. *Gli duoi fratelli rivali*, although written in the last half of the sixteenth century was not printed until 1911, when Vincenzo Spampanato edited Della Porta's *Le commedie* (2 vols., Bari, 1911), II, 195–301.

19. Jean-Antoine de Baïf, *Euvres en rime*, ed. Charles Marty-Laveaux (5 vols., Paris, 1881–90), II, 231–260.

20. The various translations of the *Orlando Furioso* as a whole are given in G. J. Ferrazzi's *Bibliografia Ariostesca* (Bassano, 1881). Aside from Visito Maurizi's Latin translation (1570), the most interesting are the French versions. An anonymous prose

translation (probably by Jean Martin or Jean de Gauttes) appeared first in 1543, with subsequent editions in 1545, '52, '55, '71, and '82. The popularity of this work is attested by the fact that there were two editions in a single year. For 1545 we find both a Lyon and a Paris imprint and, for 1555, two different Paris imprints. In this latter year there were printed two editions of the verse translation of the first fifteen *canti*, the work of Jean Fornier de Montauban. A complete verse translation by Guillaume Landré appeared in Paris in 1571, while a second prose translation, this by Gabriel Chappuys, was printed in 1576, '77, and '82, with several further editions after 1600. The first twelve canti were anonymously translated into verse and printed in two editions at Lyon in 1580. There were Spanish translations printed in 1544, '49, '54, and '58. In spite of the number of editions, few, if any, of the French translations are to be found in American libraries, and I have been unable to examine copies of the foregoing.

III

THE SIGNIFICANCE OF THE SOURCES

A detailed examination of each of the foregoing sources would clarify somewhat the transmission of the details of the plot, but such a study would be tedious and would add little to our understanding of the unity of *Much Ado*. It is demonstrable, at least on the basis of present knowledge, that no known source contains all the events and characters of Shakespeare's play. In such a case it is easy to understand the desire of scholars to posit an earlier play—either his own or someone else's—which Shakespeare revised, or to posit lost "materials lying at Shakespeare's hand." [1] It would appear that there must have been some play or tale which would bring together the seemingly diverse elements in *Much Ado*.

If, however, we read all the sources and compare them with the play, it will be apparent that the nature of the characters in the main plot is quite unlike that found in any source. Further if Hero and Claudio are understood in Elizabethan, not nineteenth- or twentieth-century terms, a definite connection between them and Benedick and Beatrice is apparent. The important thing then becomes not Shakespeare's borrowings but his "wading further," his creative reinterpretation of his sources. It will appear that Shakespeare reacted in almost antithetical fashion to the ideas and points of view expressed by the authors who preceded him in telling the story. Thus a study of the significance of the sources is a study of the ideological provenance of the story, for the characters and details of plot did not exist in vacuo; they were part of a literary tradition familiar to any Elizabethan who read anything of the literature of his age.

Even if Shakespeare did revise a play he had written some years ear-

1. D. J. Gordon, *"Much Ado About Nothing:* A Possible Source for the Hero-Claudio Plot," *Studies in Philology,* p. 284. Dr. Gordon finds in *Gli duoi fratelli rivali* a possible explanation of Borachio's puzzling line, "hear me call Margaret Hero, hear Margaret term me Claudio." Certainly this implies a mock wooing which if overheard would not deceive Claudio but would at once lead to an investigation. Dr. Gordon thinks the line is an uncorrected carry-over from the "lost materials," for in Della Porta's play there is mention of a mock love scene in which two servants will wear fine clothes and pretend to be their betters. There is, however, no suggestion that such a scene is to be witnessed; it is simply the means whereby the parasite may secure possession of the gown and the jewels which are to be used later to dupe the lover. There is no reason to be concerned, as Dr. Gordon is, because we hear nothing more of this; we are not supposed to. Nor is it quite accurate to say, "In no other of the Italian or English versions is there such a passage" (p. 286). As a matter of fact, just such a scene does occur in Ariosto. Polynesso induces Dalinda to dress in Genevra's clothes so that wooing her thus attired he may pretend to hold Genevra in his arms. It is somewhat simpler to notice this scene in connection with Borachio's statement than it is to posit lost "materials lying at Shakespeare's hand" which were influenced by a play that existed in a manuscript in Italy. *Gli duoi fratelli rivali* was first printed in 1911.

lier, the problem of Benedick and Beatrice remains. Why did he include them in this early play? Other problems must also be explained. Early or late Shakespeare represented in Hero and Claudio a relationship that has no parallel with any of the known sources. Such alteration, whenever it took place, is part of Shakespeare's purposeful construction of his play, just as is the addition of new characters.

Such addition and alteration are not, I think, the result of mere caprice. They result from Shakespeare's reaction to, and consequent reinterpretation of, the ideas and points of view expressed in the sources. To ascertain the significance of these to Shakespeare we need not examine in detail all the materials; those which indicate the salient aspects in the growth and development of the traditional viewpoint will be sufficient.

DRAMATIC VERSIONS

The extant dramatic versions are of little importance in this study since they are, with the exception of Ayrer's *Die schoene Phaenecia,* in the tradition of the "commedia erudita" which is essentially Plautine in structure. One complication follows another as the highly involved plot is unraveled and the usual stock characters—the braggart soldier, the clever servant, the parasite, and nurse—play their conventional roles. The only connection between them and Shakespeare is the fact of deception, and the form of this is unlike that found in *Much Ado.* Thematically there is little resemblance. *Il Fedele,* Fraunce's Latin translation thereof, *Victoria,* and the shortened English adaptation, *Two Italian Gentlemen,* all deal with the vengeance of a rejected lover who is denied his former pleasures. Love is amoral carnalism, and the deception is aimed at causing the death of the former mistress. The stratagem consists in having a servant emerge from Victoria's home after an assignation with the lady's maid. Sighing over his late-enjoyed pleasures he praises Victoria as their author. The husband or lover (*Two Italian Gentlemen*) believes his ears, and the inevitable complications ensue. Della Porta's *Gli duoi fratelli rivali* resembles Bandello's novella, but the rival suitors are brothers and the manner of deception varies. A servant emerges from a supposed assignation carrying the lady's robes and the gifts of her fiancé; the sight of these objects is regarded as convincing proof by the concealed lover. The fourth play, *Die schoene Phaenecia,* is adapted from Belleforest and contributes nothing to our purpose that will not be noted in a discussion of the latter's story.

Of the lost plays we know very little. It is likely that Mulcaster would have much the same approach as Beverley, while "the matter of Panecia" could have been in either the Plautine or Senecan tradition. To judge from Ronsard's comment,[2] the Fontainebleau *Genièvre* evidently fol-

2. See below, p. 20.

lowed Ariosto in point of view. These plays would undoubtedly be of great interest, but the surviving nondramatic versions well illustrate the literary tradition which underlies Shakespeare's play.

NONDRAMATIC VERSIONS

THE INFLUENCE OF ARIOSTO

All other extant versions of the story, with the exception of those of Alciat and Cinthio, belong to one of two groups: Ariosto and his imitators on the one hand, and Bandello and Belleforest on the other. The dominant influence is that of the *Orlando Furioso* which Beverley, Whetstone, and Spenser adapt and which Taillemont, Saint Gelais and De Baïf, and Harington translate. The Alciat story mentioned by Harington will not concern us, since it deals only with the defense of a woman falsely charged with adultery. Cinthio's narrative seems to be an independent adaptation from *Tirante el blanco,* for, as in the Spanish tale, the instigator of the deception is a jealous woman. Bandello's version is said by Rajna [3] and Dr. Matulka [4] to derive from Ariosto, and in this relationship we see emphasized the principle of "wading further," since the fact of a rival and the deception are the only common elements. The scene, the characters, the point of view—all these are unlike.[5]

Ariosto being a model for so many others, it will be pertinent to examine not only the facts which he presents but also the point of view from which these are related. At the end of Book IV the ubiquitous Renaldo, driven by a storm, arrives in Scotland. Arranging a rendezvous with his men, Renaldo departs in search of a worthy adventure and, at the very first abbey he visits, hears that the Princess Genevra has been condemned by the cruel law of Scotland to die at the stake unless a champion defeat her accuser, Lurcanio. He sets forth resolved to defend Genevra but is temporarily delayed when he rescues Dalinda from her would-be murderers. Continuing on his journey, Renaldo hears from Dalinda the whole sad story. As a young girl of good family she first came to court to serve Genevra, the king's daughter, and promptly fell in love with Polynesso, duke of Albany, who, she thought, loved her in return. Thus Dalinda took advantage of the fact that Genevra frequently abandoned her own

---

3. Pio Rajna, *Le fonti dell' Orlando Furioso* (Firenze, 1900), p. 149. "L'episodio del *Furioso* generà una novella del Bandello . . ."

4. *The Novels of Juan de Flores*, p. 193. ". . . the Bandello version of the story, which in its turn is based upon Ariosto."

5. It is perhaps because of these dissimilarities that Professor Gaw ("Is Shakespeare's *Much Ado* a Revised Earlier Play?" *PMLA*, p. 722) posits a lost version from which both Ariosto and Bandello derived. Professor Gaw does not mention Pio Rajna. Professor Parrott likewise thinks it unlikely that Bandello used Ariosto and mentions Weichberger's suggestion (*Jahrbuch*, XXXIV, 345) that Bandello may have seen the MS of Chariton's romance at Florence ("Two Dramatic Versions of the Slandered Bride Theme," *Joseph Quincy Adams Memorial Studies* [Washington, 1948], pp. 540–541).

bed chamber to sleep elsewhere in the castle, and by means of a rope ladder allowed Polynesso access to her in the princess' room.

But the duke was duplicitous. Although he was perfectly willing to continue the relationship with Dalinda, keeping her as his mistress, he wanted to marry Genevra. Dalinda, perforce, not only agreed but did her best to persuade the princess to love Polynesso. Genevra, however, was in love with Ariodant who, with his brother Lurcanio, had recently arrived in Scotland from Italy. The more Dalinda urged Polynesso's suit, the more Genevra loved Ariodant, and so the duke decided on villainy to separate the two. First he urged Dalinda to dress in her mistress' robes to the end that he might imagine he wooed and possessed Genevra. Then he repaired to Ariodant and in the name of the friendship that had existed between them reproached the latter for coming between him and his love. Ariodant protested, but Polynesso offered to prove that he actually enjoyed Genevra's favors, and so arrangements were made for Ariodant and Lurcanio to conceal themselves to witness the assignation. Dalinda, dressed as Genevra, let down a rope ladder which the duke ascended. Ariodant, thus deceived, made ready to kill himself but was dissuaded by Lurcanio who urged revenge. But there was no pleasure in the thought of vengeance; so our hero disappeared. Eventually a peasant brought Genevra the report that Ariodant had leapt from a high cliff into the sea where presumably he died. The peasant then repeated the somewhat cryptic couplet which the deceived lover had entrusted to him as a last message:

> Had he bene blind, he had full happie beene,
> His death should shew that he too much had seene.[6]

This news overcame Genevra, but it made Lurcanio resolve to reveal the evidence of the assignation. He did, Genevra was condemned, and Polynesso, fearing lest Dalinda reveal her part in the deception, feigned that he wished her to go to his castle and thus delivered her into the hands of his murderous henchmen.

Just as Dalinda brings Renaldo up to date, they arrive at St. Andrews, where they learn that a stranger knight has appeared as Genevra's champion to fight Lurcanio. Quickly they hasten to the lists only to discover the combat already under way, but this is soon halted by Renaldo's explanation to the king. Polynesso, denying the charges, offers to prove his truth by single combat with his accuser and is, of course, defeated. Before expiring the wicked duke manages a confession. The rest of the denouement is equally swift. The stranger knight is revealed to be Ariodant, who no sooner plunged from the cliff than he repented of his rashness and

6. *Orlando Furioso in English Heroical Verse*, Bk. V, st. 58, p. 36. I have standardized the names of the principal characters in this story and the imitations thereof to avoid possible confusion.

decided to swim for shore. Brooding over his love for Genevra he was shocked to hear of her imminent death; so he resolved to defend her even against his own brother. In short order the lovers are married; Dalinda, forgiven, repairs to a nunnery, and Ariosto hastens back to Ruggiero whom he has left in mid-air aboard the Hippogriff.

The Genevra episode is like many another extraneous tale which Ariosto introduced to adorn his romantic epic. It has no hidden meaning nor any relation to the characters or main events of the *Orlando;* it is a narrative which pleases by its recital of events. The events are complicated; Polynesso's stratagem is clever; there is a nice irony in Lurcanio's praiseworthy attempt to avenge his brother; and there is a fine deus ex machina denouement. As narrative it has everything that one could ask, but it is primarily the story of Dalinda and not that of Ariodant and Genevra. Ronsard makes this quite clear when he writes:

> Quand voirrons nous un autre Polynesse
> Tromper Dalinde?[7]

The deceived Dalinda narrates the major portion of the story; her deception by Polynesso is what is important to her, for, as she says in almost her first words to Renaldo,

> Loue should preuaile, iust anger to asswage,
> If loue bring death, whereto can women trust?
> Yet loue did breed my danger and my feare,
> As you shall heare if you will giue me eare.[8]

Genevra, though the titular heroine, occupies a most inferior position in the narrative; she, Ariodant, and Lurcanio are of importance only as puppets in the narrative sequence whose main characters are Polynesso and Dalinda. Certainly Genevra and Ariodant are in love, but their love story is not what Ariosto sought to emphasize.

With Beverley there is a complete shift in emphasis, for he does tell us the tale of the two lovers. There is no thrusting into the midst of things for him; he begins at the beginning with Ariodant and Lurcanio in Italy hearing news of the surpassing beauty of the fair Genevra, daughter of the king of Scotland. Forthwith they set out on the perilous journey. On their arrival at the Scotch court they are greeted with suspicion; the king fears they may be spies. All is soon set right, however, for during a hunt Lurcanio rescues the king from a wounded lion. Having thus managed to beat out some two hundred and fifty lines, Beverley has his lovers meet for the first time and, of course, "Venus child hath tainted

---

7. *Oeuvres complètes de Pierre Ronsard,* ed. Paul Laumonier (8 vols., Paris, 1914–19), III, 300. Here Ronsard is appealing to Queen Catherine to return to Paris, and he is describing the pleasures which the court had known before her departure. Among them was the play *Genièvre.*

8. *Orlando Furioso,* Bk. V, st. 6, p. 32.

two with his sharpe persing dart." Neither believes that the other can possibly reciprocate the love that torments each. How can Ariodant aspire to the daughter of a king, and how can a princess look with favor on a mere errant knight? With the affair at this seeming impasse, Beverley describes at great length the love sickness of the pair. Their sufferings are obvious, but the cause is a mystery to everyone. The fires of love so rage that the victims are forced to take to their respective beds where they find no rest or surcease. In fact, Ariodant is brought to such dire straits that he beats his head upon the floor to obtain relief. Finally, through the medium of a dream the lovers become aware of their mutual affection. The dream could have arrived much earlier, but then Beverley would have deprived himself of the opportunity to dilate on such a fine theme as love sickness.

Such thematic development is Beverley's artistic purpose: the narrative exists as a framework which he adorns with rhetorical elaborations. Principally his theme is love, and the stereotypes of love behavior are his subjects; but nothing that can be described in alliterative clichés is neglected. Whereas Ariosto canters briskly, Beverley jogs and ambles. Where Ariosto alludes briefly to Italy as the home of Ariodant and Lurcanio, Beverley expands in a large number of doggerel couplets on the reasons why the two brothers left home, the details of their journey, their reception in Scotland, and Lurcanio's rescue of the king. In the same fashion Ariosto's suggestion that friendship had existed between Ariodant and Polynesso is amply developed. For pages these two discuss friendship and the proper course to follow when there is a conflict between love and friendship. In short, Beverley, in retelling an old story, has spared no pains in "wading further" and plumbing all possible depths, despite his Uriah Heep disparagement of his offering as a "rude Booke."

Love, however, is the poet's main concern. When, after the dream, Ariodant enlists the help of Genevra's maid and conceals a letter in the princess' prayer book, one might expect that the story would progress, but it does not. Here is still another opportunity to explore the reactions of lovers. We must hear Genevra's soliloquy of joy on reading the letter, as well as Ariodant's when he receives an answer.

It is this fondness for rhetorical elaboration which leads Beverley not only to develop and expand those narrative details found in Ariosto but to add others. None of the details of the inception of love, the sickness, the dream, or the letters exchanged are in the *Orlando;* they are original with Beverley, but they are not novel. All of these events are characteristic of the literary patterns of the time. Brooke adds just such details to his version of the Romeo-Juliet story and the same type of thing is to be found throughout Geoffrey Fenton's *Certain Tragical Discourses.* It might be possible to find some novella or romance which exhibited now one, now another of the details that Beverley adds, but the necessary search has not seemed worth while. Why Beverley adds to his original is abundantly clear : he wants to include everything that pertains in any way to a love story. Thus he has Genevra arrange a meeting with Ariodant at a well-hidden olive tree, since lovers should have trysts and since what is said on such occasions is well worth recording. The device of the letters concealed in the prayer book and attendance at divine service as a means of exchanging the book is of precisely the same origin.

Nor can our author be content with the deception as he found it in Ariosto. Any good love story must include a "suspicion" passage wherein the lover makes abundant moan about the duplicity of women.[9] So that Ariodant may thus lament, Beverley introduces the episode of the ring. Genevra prizes highly a diamond ring given her by Ariodant. In order to prove to Ariodant that Genevra is faithless, Polynesso offers to produce the ring which he swears Genevra will give him. Dalinda secures the ring while the princess sleeps, Polynesso shows it to Ariodant who reacts in the proper fashion, and while our hero languishes in doleful moan Polynesso sends it back to Dalinda, so that Genevra will not be aware of even its temporary absence. Dalinda, of course, is motivated by her love for Polynesso and his promises to marry her. It is true that she is the duke's mistress, but unlike her namesake in the *Orlando* she is unwilling to continue this relationship any longer than necessary. It is again a promise of marriage which induces her to dress in Genevra's robes. Polynesso proposes to woo her in this guise so that he may in vicarious fashion triumph over the disdainful Genevra and thus become emotionally free to marry Dalinda. Similarly she willingly accompanies the murderous henchmen because they are to escort her to the duke's home where the marriage is to take place.

Beverley has no intention of diminishing Dalinda's role simply because he has emphasized the loves of Ariodant and Genevra. The deceived Dalinda is used to produce pathos as she vainly trusts the duke and hopes continually to be made an honest woman. Her big scene occurs when, rescued by Renaldo, she returns to the city and to the lists. There she confesses all and denounces her seducer. Whereas Ariosto hurried through his denouement and gave the explanation to Renaldo, Beverley made the most of the pathos and rhetoric of the situation.

Some ten years later when George Whetstone dealt with the story the love conventions had become more sophisticated, as we shall see from a consideration of *The Discourse of Rinaldo and Giletta*.[10] As has been shown elsewhere,[11] the first half of this narrative is an imitation of Gas-

9. George Gascoigne interpolated in *The Adventures of Master F.J.* just such a passage which he took from Ariosto's *Cinque canti. A Hundreth Sundrie Flowres*, pp. 82–84, 253.

10. See above, n. 17, p. 14.

11. C. T. Prouty, "Elizabethan Fiction: Whetstone's *Rinaldo and Giletta* and Grange's *The Golden Aphroditis*," *Studies in Honor of A. H. R. Fairchild, University of Missouri Studies*, XXI, No. 1 (Columbia, 1946), 133–143.

coigne's *The Adventures of Master F.J.*, while the remainder is a free adaptation of the Genevra episode. This division into two parts is quite natural, since it is based on the contemporary idea of the typical love story which takes a great deal of time to get the lovers through the initial stages of love at first sight, the fear that the love is not reciprocated, the consequent love sickness, to the joyful meeting where mutual affection is confessed and the sequent idyl of perfect bliss. When an author has reached this point he must introduce some complication or his story automatically comes to an end. Whetstone, even as Beverley, Gascoigne, Grange, and others, takes refuge in the conventional.

In this sort, in absence, with letters, in presence, with lokes, signes, and louing greetings, now & then, with a stollen kisse interioyned, for a space these louers, yᵉ one the other delighted. But (oh) I sighe to report, how soudainly fortune threatened the spoile of their desires, yea whē they thought themselues of her fauor most assured, such are the chaunges & chaunces of loue. But sith her thretning (after a number of griefes by these two louers suffered) tourned into grace: with more willingnes, I enter into discourse of their sorrowes as followeth.¹²

These sorrows, at least those enjoyed by Rinaldo, arrive suddenly, for our hero is stricken with an ague which keeps him in his bed where he has nothing better to think on than "feareful fancies, continually dreading how that his absence would turne his Ladies loue to mislyking." Ironically enough, these fancies are realized, but not because of any rejection of Rinaldo by Giletta. Very abruptly a new suitor is introduced whose presence radically alters the situation. Since Giletta is the daughter of the lord of Bologna, and since Rinaldo is "a gentleman of better qualities and shape, then either of birth or living," there is little hope of parental consent to a marriage. Frizaldo represents the approved suitor of good birth and considerable possessions. In a way the situation in which Giletta finds herself is similar to that facing Juliet in love with Romeo but urged and finally commanded to marry Paris. Giletta is either not as much in love as Juliet or else she is a more dutiful daughter who does not dream of anything so scandalous as a secret marriage; all she can do is temporize.

Unfortunately Frizaldo is acute in the presence of love's aura, so that he soon perceives the true relationship between Rinaldo and Giletta. When the latter visits the sick Rinaldo, she carries with her a posy of gilly flowers whose properties are "that about whose head they bee bestowed, the same wighte shal not bee much frighted with feareful fancies." ¹³ Thus comforted, Rinaldo gives to his lady a branch of rosemary. The meaning of this exchange might well elude the modern reader,

12. "The Castle of Delight," *The Rocke of Regard*, pp. 39–40.
13. *Ibid.*, p. 41.

but Frizaldo, ever alert and subtle, perceives its true significance, and as the company make their way home he tells Giletta, "Well . . . you were best to perfecte your delighte, to weare a Rose with your Rosemarie, meaninge the first letters of those two flowers, aunsweared her louers name, *Roberto Rinaldo*." [14] Alarmed by this perception, Giletta becomes subtle in turn. She must not anger Frizaldo lest her secret love be openly revealed, so she determines "to feede [him] with courteous delayes: *Rinaldo,* whom in deede she honoured, shee determined in heart to loue, and in showe to hate, thinking by this meanes that she should extinguish & quench Frizaldo's ielous suspicion." [15] Such a plan is all very well provided Rinaldo is aware of it; but if he is not, his "feareful fancies" will be confirmed. And soon they are. Restored to health, our lover hastens to visit his mistress whom "hee found . . . dallying with a fresh gallant: On him shee would not vouchsafe to looke: Yea, if on occasion hee saluted her by the name of his mystresse, very disdainfully and scornefully, or not at all shee aunsweared him: On him shee frowned with a curst countenaunce: On his enimie shee fleared with a delightsome fauour." [16] When the courtiers add the news that Frizaldo is to marry Giletta, Rinaldo retires to prepare a doleful lament which he sings under Giletta's window that very evening. As the words, set to "a very sollem note," reach Giletta's ears the identity of the singer is recognized not only by her but by the rival as well, since Frizaldo is in Giletta's chamber. The hateful villain determines on "slye policie" and addresses Giletta "by the name of his subiect: Who duetifully aunswered him, with ye title of her souereigne," [17] because to reject the gambit would be tantamount to an open admission of her love for Rinaldo.

This is indeed a most sophisticated form of deception; but there can be no doubt, for Rinaldo has heard with his own ears those fearsome words, "subject and sovereign," and knows only too well what they mean. The game of love has become devious and subtle, and Whetstone records the development; but he does not, however, reject or alter all the elements of his original. For example, we soon discover Frizaldo promising to marry Rosina, Giletta's maid, in order to gain her aid and her silence, just as Polynesso promised to marry Dalinda.

As in Beverley, we are treated to a twofold deception. Not only is Rinaldo tricked by Frizaldo's subtlety, he is also deluded by a false message. Giletta knows what those words "sovereign and subject" meant to Rinaldo, so to explain her behavior and confirm her love she attempts to send him a message concealed in an apple, but Rosina, who is to give the apple to Rinaldo, reports the device to Frizaldo who substitutes a note flatly

14. *Ibid.,* p. 42.
15. *Ibid.,* p. 43.
16. *Ibid.*
17. *Ibid.,* p. 45.

rejecting the lover. At this point the story returns to the original pattern: Rinaldo jumps into the sea after having entrusted to a passerby a message for Giletta, which echoes Ariodant's message to Genevra and is equally succinct.

> Giletta false of faith Rinaldo nipt so nye,
> That lo he chose before his time, in stremes of Poo to dy.[18]

Like Ariodant, Rinaldo is no sooner immersed than he repents his rash decision and makes for land, but even though he is thus alive, his happy reunion with Giletta cannot be achieved by Ariosto's means. There is no accusation of unchastity nor is there any "cruel law of Bologna"; but Whetstone does not lack either invention or an awareness of fine pathetical scenes. The disconsolate Rinaldo, after a brief sojourn in the wilds, again decides on suicide but this time resolves to use a dagger and spill his blood underneath Giletta's window. Ere he dies he plans to use this blood to write on the wall a brief poem which he has composed. These romantic resolutions so magnificently anticipate the manifold suicide thoughts of young Werther that we are not at all surprised when we read that, arrived at the fatal spot and "finding his enterprise (by reason of ye dead time of night) unlikely to be troubled, before he executed this tragedie" he resolves on a lengthy speech of farewell. There is, of course, great method in this romantic madness, for his groans awake Giletta who hastens outside for a heroic scene of recognition.

The end is now in sight. Giletta pretends to favor Frizaldo but confesses to her father that she is somewhat hesitant to proceed to marriage, since she had promised herself to Rinaldo. Father obliges by issuing a proclamation giving her to Rinaldo, if he turns up within the month. With Giletta seemingly assured him, Frizaldo is in difficulties with Rosina whom he has promised to marry; but his ingenuity saves him. He tells Rosina that he is only playing a game of vengeance: Giletta has treated him so badly that he desires the great satisfaction of rejecting her at the altar.[19] Rosina is to be conveyed to his home where he will hasten, directly he has enjoyed his triumph. Rinaldo, like his namesake in Ariosto, rescues the maid from the murderers, and we hasten to Bologna where Rosina confesses. Subsequently, Rinaldo, after killing Frizaldo, marries Giletta.

Truly Whetstone has reinterpreted his sources in a most novel manner. As with Beverley, love has been his theme but it has been handled in the latest fashion. The newest refinements and subtleties are all displayed with a liberal dash of melodramatic seasoning. Frizaldo really

18. *Ibid.*, p. [49] which is erroneously paginated "33" in the Huntington copy I have used.

19. Had Shakespeare read this version, he might have derived his altar-renunciation idea from it.

becomes the nineteenth-century villain when Rinaldo defies him with, "Notorious varlet (spoyled of all humanitie) I am he that wil mainteine her sayings [Rosina's confession about the apple] true, and in reuenge of thy trecherie, will (I trust) soone seperate thy condēned soule (w^{t}out speedie repentance) from thy carren body." [20] The *Orlando Furioso* has no such lines as these, nor does any other version of the story; they are Whetstone's own contribution.

The remaining English versions need not detain us long: Harington translates without addition, and Spenser [21] adapts the story to suit a very particular purpose of his own. When Guyon first sees him, Phedon is being dragged along the ground by Furor, and the story he tells, when freed, illustrates the results of rage. The crux of Spenser's version is the deception which rouses rage in the deceived Phedon and leads him to kill his innocent fiancée, Claribell. The stratagem is a variation of the Ariosto device; Philemon, the false friend, woos Pryene, Claribell's maid, and telling her that she is as beautiful as her mistress induces her to dress in the now familiar robes. Having arranged for Phedon to hide in a secret corner, Philemon reappears disguised as a groom to play out the love scene. The enraged Phedon kills Claribell and after Pryene's confession has revealed the stratagem, he kills Philemon. At this point Pryene flies and while pursuing her, Phedon is captured by Furor. Thus in Spenser's handling of it the story becomes an exemplum showing the results of rage as one kind of intemperance. In keeping with this purpose Spenser has cut the story to its barest essentials in accordance with his reinterpretation for a definite end. Exactly the same type of thing may be seen in Spenser's adaptation [22] of the familiar story of Dom Diego to suit the state of Timias, who despairs when Belphoebe discovers him with Amoret. Rejected by Belphoebe, Timias builds himself a solitary cabin in a gloomy wood where he laments his sad case in bad verse. There is much more to the original, but Spenser has used only that portion which suits his purpose.

THE INFLUENCE OF BANDELLO

Turning to the Italian and French versions, we see again great freedom in the reinterpretation of sources. Bandello's prefatory remarks suggest his point of view and consequently help to explain the divergence of his story of Timbreo and Fenecia from that of Ariodant and Genevra. The bishop of Agen, dedicating each of his novelle to some worthy and noble person, atttempts to make his dedications both flattering and apt.

20. *The Rocke of Regard*, p. 60.
21. See above, n. 1, p. 11.
22. *Faerie Queene*, Bk. IV, Canto 7, sts. 33–47. *The Poetical Works of Edmund Spenser*, pp. 248–249.

In the present instance [23] Bandello is in good form : he and Signor Lucio Attelano while on their way to Gazuolo passed very near the castle of Signora Cecilia Gallerana, Countess Bergamina ; so, not wishing to commit sacrilege, they stopped to pay their respects to the lady. Inevitably the company turned to storytelling, and Attelano's narrative not only greatly pleased the entire company but was commended at length by the countess. Although he lacks "the sweet speech of our resourceful and eloquent Attelano," Bandello decides to write out the story so that he may present the manuscript as a gift to the countess.

Why this noble lady praised the story and how Sir John Harington found it "a pretie comicall matter" are suggested by the description which directly prefaces it. "Signor Scipioni Attelano tells how the Signor Timbreo di Cardona, being with King Piers of Aragon in Messina, fell in love with Fenicia Leonata and of the various happenings sent by Fortune which occurred before he took her for wife." [24] A love story is a staple commodity but this is a love story with complications or, in the modern idiom, a love story with "angles," and such angles were highly esteemed by both the countess and Sir John. Although ingenuity of plot construction is not highly esteemed in our time, it was an obvious selling point in the Renaissance, as "the various happenings" are what enhance the worth of the story of Timbreo and Fenicia for Bandello and the countess. Assuredly Harington admired the same qualities in the Genevra episode.

Although it would seem that Bandello was indebted to Ariosto for the fact of deception and the theme of friendship so casually mentioned in connection with Polynesso and Ariodant, his happenings are so different and his point of view so much his own that his story may be regarded as almost a separate entity.[25] The character represented by Dalinda in Ariosto is eliminated, since here the action arises from the conflict of love and friendship and there is no deceived woman. Timbreo, the wealthy young favorite of the king, and his sworn brother Girondo both love Fenicia, a young woman of inferior economic and social station. Hearing that the marriage has been arranged, Girondo in desperation plans to deceive his friend who he hopes will then reject Fenicia, so that thus the way may be clear for him to woo and win her. Girondo, unlike Polynesso, does not appear at all in the deception. Instead he enlists the aid of "a young courtier, a man of slight intelligence, one to whom evil is more pleasing than good," [26] and it is this character who tells Timbreo that Fenicia is profligate, offers proof, arranges the rendezvous, and manages the whole affair. The deception itself is quite weak: Timbreo sees an anonymous lover approach a deserted wing of Fenicia's home with serv-

23. *La Prima Parte De Le Novelle Del Bandello*, fols. 149ʳ–166ʳ.
24. *Ibid.*, fol. 150ʳ. The translation is by the present author.
25. See above, p. 18.
26. *La Prima Parte De Le Novelle Del Bandello*, fol. 151ᵛ.

ants who put in place the ladder they have been carrying. The lover admonishes his servants that on previous occasions the considerable noise which they had made with the ladder had disturbed Fenicia, who feared discovery. Thus is Timbreo convinced, and the results are what we expect, since Girondo has allowed love to triumph over friendship. In any medieval or Renaissance treatment of the love-*vs.*-friendship theme, trouble invariably results from the domination of love. Let friendship once reappear as the prime force and everything is set right. So it is in Chaucer's "Knight's Tale" and so it is in *Two Gentlemen of Verona;* and thus it is in the story at hand. Timbreo denounces Fenicia's unchastity in a letter to her father, and although the reaction of both Lionato and his daughter is that Timbreo is seizing upon an excuse to avoid marriage with an inferior, she does swoon, is thought dead, and recovers only after the news of her death has been spread abroad.

The plan to conceal Fenicia at her uncle's home in the country while a funeral is conducted over an empty casket is typical of the Realpolitik in domestic affairs which characterizes the story. Although Fenicia has lost one husband, her father's quick wits see a way to allow her the possibility of securing another. The girl is to live in the country for two or three years where she will grow and change somewhat in looks. Assuming a new name and emerging from seclusion, she will never be connected with the defamed Fenicia and may thus be married off. The morality of this is consonant with that of Timbreo's love. Our hero falls in love it is true, but his passion is not of a romantic persuasion. All he desires is to seduce the girl who, being well and carefully brought up, realizes this fact quite clearly, for to all "the letters, messengers, and embassages which he sent her she never otherwise replied than that she was resolved to preserve her virginity inviolate for him who should be given her as husband." [27] Needless to say Fenicia's tactics are as successful as they are some two centuries later when practiced by Mistress Pamela Andrews. Like Squire B., Don Timbreo is forced to purchase pleasure at the price of matrimony. These aspects of love and marriage are passed over rather briefly by Bandello, not because he wishes to conceal anything, but for the very simple reason that such were the accepted customs of his world, and the pattern was axiomatic not only for him but for his readers.

With Fenicia presumed defunct we are ready for the revelation of the truth; Girondo repents his rash act, confesses his sin, and is absolved when friendship assumes supremacy. In a most pathetic scene before the tomb wherein he supposes Fenicia's body to lie, Girondo bares his breast and offering a dagger to Timbreo beseeches the latter to make an end to one who has wronged him. Of course Timbreo does nothing of the sort; instead there is general lamentation during the course of which our hero says that he will never seek vengeance against his brother. Little remains

27. *Ibid.,* fol. 150ᵛ.

but to work out the details whereby Timbreo and Fenicia may be reunited and a wife found for Girondo. This is accomplished by having Timbreo render what amendment he can to Lionato by swearing to marry none but a wife of Lionato's choosing. After a year's interval the prospective wife is produced, her identity is revealed, and a double wedding is celebrated whereby Timbreo at last has Fenicia, and Girondo is quite content to be paired off with her younger sister, Belfiore.

Throughout, Bandello's concern is with his narrative, and he allows few if any interruptions. Whether or no Signor Attelano's tale was the source, it should be remembered that Bandello was recording a story that either had been or could be delivered orally.[28] Thus while the conventions are observed, their observance is but perfunctory. Timbreo is a lover and as such he falls in love in the usual literary fashion: the blaze of Beauty has entered his eyes to travel thence to his heart where it creates a fire. All this is assumed, for when we meet Timbreo the fire has flourished apace, and now we learn that further gazing upon Fenicia has increased the conflagration. With such topics as Fenicia's reaction to the charge of unchastity, and the confession of Girondo, Bandello allows himself more scope, but his interest is not to ornament with rhetoric. Since these scenes are filled with implicit pathos, the author is well aware of the value of such emotion in a story and does his best to realize the potentialities. Even in an oral narrative pathos does not hinder the flow of action; instead, through indirect means, it affords an opportunity for recalling the happy past and indicating the necessarily joyous future. All will end well; it must; so pathos may be said to whet the appetite: how is this journey's end to be reached?

On the other hand, neither Belleforest nor Beverley is interested in narration as an end itself. To these men the narrative is but a means whereby they may display their own ability in the art of words. A possible and easy analogy in our time is to be found in the continued spate of musical adaptations of plays. *The Taming of the Shrew* is but a peg on which to hang the music and lyrics of Cole Porter. So with Belleforest: Bandello may have told a perfectly good story but really the simple fellow had no idea of style nor what constituted "good writing." Actually the difference between Bandello and Belleforest is the difference between an oral version and that written by a second- or third-rate man who fancies himself as a literary figure and a philosopher. Whereas Bandello was a sophisticated teller of stories, Belleforest, Beverley, and such adaptors

28. Cf. John Addington Symonds, *The Renaissance in Italy* (Modern Library Ed., New York, n.d.), II, 201, 203. "The narrator went straight to his object, which was to arrest the attention, stimulate the curiosity, gratify the sensual instincts, excite the laughter, or stir the tender emotions of his audience by some fantastic, extraordinary, voluptuous, comic, or pathetic incident. . . . The student of contemporary Italian customs will glean abundant information from these pages; the student of human nature gathers little except reflections on the morals of sixteenth-century society."

of Belleforest as Painter and Fenton were harbingers in their own countries. They were not the products of a rather highly developed society; they were aping the work of such a civilization and were trying to improve according to their ideas. Such improvement was nothing new; it may be found in a comparison of Seneca with Euripides. The Roman thought he was doing a much better job, and his readers most probably agreed with him. Similarly in a later time Nahum Tate thought that he was improving *King Lear*. Easy as it is for us to laugh at such "improvements," we can, if we are interested, learn a great deal about the tastes and standards of the improvers and their ages by noting the nature of the alterations.

Just as Beverley "improved" on Ariosto, so did Belleforest "improve" on Bandello, and there is close correspondence between the literary interests of the two. The Frenchman, for example, produces the usual cliché of the inception of love. The blaze of Fénicie's beauty has entered Timbrée's eyes and has traveled thence to his heart where it has kindled a raging fire. Timbrée, arrayed in all his finery marches up and down in front of Fénicie's home, feeding his flames by glimpsing her face and rousing interest in her heart, since naturally no young girl could be oblivious to such a personage. To round out this fulsome treatment of love Belleforest has his heroine accept and read both a letter and a Spanish song of some one hundred and thirty-five lines. Another elaboration is a new character, the nurse who is only too willing to assist Timbrée in his attempts at seduction. It is she who carries the messages and who recites to Fénicie an exhaustive account of the noble lord's sufferings. But she in turn is forced to listen when the heroine affirms at great length her duty to her parents and her resolve to love none but the man whom her parents give her as husband or whom God has reserved for her lord and spouse.

Belleforest finds other opportunities for rhetorical digression. A long passage on the malignancy of destiny follows upon the announcement of the wedding, for the count is brought to the usual decision of paying the high price of matrimony. Similarly Timbrée, waiting for the deception to take place, muses on the subject of the frailty of woman. Whenever there is a chance to spin out a passage and thus demonstrate his literary ability, the Frenchman is both ready and willing. The instigator of the deception, whom Bandello described in a very few words, becomes in Belleforest a true Machiavel.

. . . a man well disposed to evil doing, a man as honest as any of those who live by their wits in Paris, having no other business than to murder or give false witness, provided one pour money into their purses. This gallant, found by Gironde, was as fine a courtier as one could wish, a man of good spirit, but one who always devoted himself to evil, a dissembler, a faithless, indolent sychophant who cared for nothing but present gain; in short, as shrewd and cunning a rascal as there was in the Court of Arragon.[29]

The development of this character and the addition of the nurse represent a definite enlargement of the story, but they do not alter Bandello's pattern. On the other hand, Belleforest's emphasis on the jargon and clichés of love does tend to create a new atmosphere wherein Timbrée passes from the carnal lover to the romantic. When the count decides to marry Fénicie, he is moved not by the urgency of physical desire but by a realization of her worth and by an understanding of the nature of true love. Her innate goodness realizes no "other love than that which virtue begets, nourishes and consummates," and so Timbrée abandons "the mad pursuit of love" which had enthralled him and resolves to find true love in matrimony. Such views find no expression in Bandello; they are not of his world. Only in Belleforest and in the Englishmen, Beverley and Whetstone, do we find this acceptance of romantic love culminating in marriage. The new morality as expressed by Spenser in the person of Britomart was not a sudden development; it appears, as we note, some years before *The Faerie Queene*.

Thus in retrospect we see that the story has been altered considerably during the course of its successive redactions during the century. The original interest in narration has given way to an interest in various accretions, some purely rhetorical and others which express certain fashionable stereotypes. With Ariosto and Bandello the love of hero and heroine is merely an accepted fact, a necessary part of the plot, a raison d'être for introducing a neat deception device, which was pleasing because of its ingenuity and the complications which it entrained. To the sequent adaptors, Belleforest, Beverley, and Whetstone, "Love" is the essential and it is about love that they wish to write. Naturally they use the familiar jargon of the Petrarchan tradition, but such language and such ideas were not hackneyed to them or to their readers. Furthermore, their readers enjoyed not only the language of love but also elaborate accounts of the subtleties of love behavior.

Aside from Tottel's *Songes and Sonettes,* only the *Eglogs, Epytaphes, & Sonettes* of Barnabe Googe had appeared before Beverley wrote his poem. By 1576, when *The Rocke of Regard* was printed, both Gascoigne and Turbervile had published works which exhibited the conceits of love; but when we think of the flood tide that flowed in the 1580's we realize that Beverley and Whetstone were among the first small waves. Lyly was immensely popular because he catered to a public interested in all the ways of love, and this public was not soon satisfied, as the spate of Euphuistic romances and bad verse testifies. Following these came the end-

29. Belleforest, *Le Troisième Tome Des Histoires Tragiques,* fols. 488ᵛ–489ʳ. The translation is that of the present author.

less sonnet sequences with their endless refinements of love conceits. By the close of the century printers, publishers, and authors had come close to sating the popular demand, and Shakespeare's attitude toward his source materials must be viewed in the light of this exploitation of love jargon and love behavior. Shakespeare's specific borrowings may, as has been said, be observed and documented, but to comprehend his use of certain facts, his rejections, his alterations, and his additions we must see the raw materials in their proper milieu. It was thus that Shakespeare saw them. This, let it be repeated, does not mean that the dramatist carefully read any or all of the different stories which have been noted, or that he sat down to write with them near at hand.[30] Instead, the significance of the foregoing survey is that we have observed a variety of reactions to a single story—reactions by men who shared an attitude toward life. That attitude rested upon a variety of assumptions and axioms which were not recorded but which survive only by implication in the writings of these men.[31] To recover in some measure at least a part of this attitude has been our purpose, since it is a guide to Shakespeare's handling of the same material.

30. If it is difficult sometimes to prove what Shakespeare read, it is impossible to prove what he *heard*. Unfortunately, there was no reporter to take down the conversations in the Mermaid Tavern or in the Globe Theatre, and thus the modern critic is unable to cope with what might be considered a vast store of source material in the generic sense: that is, hearsay. But we should not forget that even as our knowledge is partly composed of odd bits of information, misinformation, rumor, gossip, and humorous anecdote which we hear daily, but which we seldom see in print, so, too, must Shakespeare have "acquired" a miscellany of fact which is intangible to us. Our reaction to such intangibles is often the root of our prejudices, good or bad. We can never know what tales Shakespeare heard over and above the ones he read, but it would be unfair to deny that he, any less than ourselves, reacted to what he heard or read, and it is my belief that in trying to perceive his reactions we come closer to knowing the man than by adhering too minutely to the safety of the tangible.

31. Jacob Ayrer's *Die schoene Phaenicia* is most interesting in this connection, for it reveals the popularity of the jargon and clichés in Germany, but Ayrer's attempts at such elaboration are so old-fashioned that they would have been regarded as very crude stuff by an English audience. The play is introduced by Venus who is angry with Count Tymborus whom she has been unable to subdue even though other warriors have fallen before her assaults. Fortunately, Cupid arrives with a fresh supply of arrows and obligingly wounds Tymborus. This representation of a cliché with actual mythological figures would have been possible in the early 1580's in England, but even then it would have been archaic. Still, the important thing is the proof which this affords of the general European preoccupation with artificial love conceits.

IV

THE PLAY

ALTERATIONS IN THE PLOT

Roger Ascham devotes a considerable section of *The Scholemaster* to a discussion of imitation as a means of acquiring skill in the writing of Latin.[1] A part of this analyzes Erasmus' suggestion that much is to be learned by comparing the work of Demosthenes and "Tullie"; "that is, to write out and ioyne together, where the one doth imitate the other." "*Erasmus* wishe is good," says Ascham, "but surelie, it is not good enough." A mere assemblage of such sentences "were but a colde helpe, to the encrease of learning."[2] What Ascham desires is a thorough comparison which he indicates in topical outline.[3]

1. *Tullie* reteyneth thus moch of the matter, thies sentences, thies wordes:
2. This and that he leaueth out, which he doth wittelie to this end and purpose.
3. This he addeth here.
4. This he diminisheth there.
5. This he ordereth thus, with placing that here, not there.
6. This he altereth and changeth, either, in propertie of wordes in forme of sentence, in substance of the matter, or in one, or other conuenient circumstance of the authors present purpose. In thies fewe rude English wordes, are wrapt vp all the necessarie tooles and instrumentes, wherewith trewe *Imitation* is rightlie wrought withall in any tonge.

If we accept these criteria they will be useful to us, since they represent the means by which a learned and intelligent Elizabethan would have approached a comparison of a Shakespearean play with its sources. We should note the wideness of Ascham's view and his concern with the purpose of the author, for whatever be our view of the literature of the past—whether we approach it in a pure and timeless state or intend to reinterpret it for our own age—we may find some value in attempting to understand the author's purpose in his own age. We may feel strongly, for example, that Shakespeare was a poet forced by the exigencies of the time to write for the theater; but if we are to avoid a critical anarchy wherein the only truth is to be "so many men, so many minds," the initial

1. *English Works of Roger Ascham*, ed. W. A. Wright (Cambridge, 1904), pp. 264–279.
2. *Ibid.*, p. 267.
3. *Ibid.*, pp. 267–268.

fact of purpose must be a guide to our analysis and a gentle restraint upon our fancy.

Perhaps the clearest indication that Shakespeare has in mind a somewhat different purpose than any of the previous tellers of the tale is his alteration of the substance of the plot. Whereas hitherto the deception plot had been put in motion by a rival lover, usually a friend of the hero, in *Much Ado* a new and unrelated character is introduced for this purpose. At first glance we may be inclined to rely on stage convention as an explanation; Don John is a Machiavel, and because such a character was then popular on the stage Shakespeare altered the plot to put him in. This might be satisfactory enough if Shakespeare always altered with such a free and careless hand; but since he does not, it may be well to credit him with more thought and purpose than such a conclusion would imply and to judge the material that is rejected by this alteration. For example, in all the sources except Whetstone's *Rinaldo and Giletta,* the rival's friendship with the hero is important in varying degrees. Girondo or Gironde is forced by remorse and friendship to reveal his villainy. Friendship not only preserves his life but makes possible his forgiveness. These are important elements of plot, productive as they are of such scenes as that before the tomb when Girondo bares his breast and offers Timbreo a dagger. Surely these are good elements of dramatic situation which would play well on the stage. In the other descent, that from Ariosto, friendship has less connection with plot. Polynesso uses his friendship for Ariodant as the excuse for revealing his own fictitious success with Genevra, and thus his falsity is enhanced; but otherwise there is little dramatic value in the situation. There is, however, a real opportunity for rhetorical elaboration of the theme, as we have seen in Beverley. The Elizabethan world was sufficiently familiar with the classical definition of friendship to enable Shakespeare to elaborate on the subject. But in spite of his fondness for the theme in the sonnets, Shakespeare is not interested in it for the plot or the rhetoric of this play; he rejects it, and I would suggest that there are two discernible reasons for the deletion.

Although there is no categorical explanation of Shakespeare's attitude in the sonnets, the possible conventionality or artificiality of the friendship motif must not be overlooked. Greene and Lyly, of Shakespeare's immediate predecessors, used it and presented it within the framework of their artificial and bookish worlds. Eumenides resolving his affection in favor of Endymion over Semele is thus able to read the message in the magic fountain and so to effect the release of his friend. The love of Euphues and Philautus for Lucilla, the complications which ensue, and the final reconciliation of the friends afford Lyly excellent opportunities for sententious reflection. Greene works over the familiar ground in *Tullies Love,* as does Lodge in *Euphues Shadow,* and always the rhetorical passages have the same general theme, and always friendship triumphs. This patterned cliché was legitimate subject matter for the sophisticated world which was certainly the audience for Lyly's plays, his novels, and the imitations thereof. It was to just such a world that E.K.'s note on the love of Hobbinol and Colin was addressed. With a great show of learning E.K. portrays the affection of these two as nonsensual and even like the love of Socrates "who sayth, that in deede he loued Alcybiades extremely, yet not Alcybiades person, but hys soule, which is Alcybiades owne selfe." [4] Within the framework of the pastoral convention which the Euphuists aped and within the artificial and stereotyped conceits of the sonnet sequences, this sort of thing is acceptable. We may with some justice imagine Spenser and other undergraduates engaged in a most serious discussion of this fascinating topic, with or without Harvey in attendance. The abstract, and particularly the abstract as found in books, has a perennial fascination for youth and other sophisticates removed from experience. Here are fine bones to gnaw upon while the cup goes round and the candles gutter. Youth, with its resiliency, will shrug off the memory of such talk, while the older dabblers will count it among their gambits; but those who aspire to "high" life and "deep" thoughts will be the only ones to take it seriously. So, I suggest, it was with this idea in Renaissance England. Courtiers could worry the subject for a careless hour, but few seriously limited or controlled their actions because of sworn brotherhood.

It was, in view of the foregoing, no accident that one of the first plays written by William Shakespeare was *The Two Gentlemen of Verona* which accepted so seriously the literary conventions of the love-*vs.*-friendship theme that the critics still argue vehemently about its ending. If we will judge by the other literary treatments of this idea, we will have no difficulty with Valentine's seemingly quixotic gift to Proteus of "all that was mine in Silvia." We may say that Valentine was a fool, and it may have been that many an Elizabethan would have agreed; but Shakespeare could defend himself, even as Ben Jonson did, by blaming his audience for being ignorant and unaware of the literary tradition which justified him. According to literary precept Valentine did the proper and correct thing: friendship should always be greater than love.

But it so happened that Shakespeare was not of Ben Jonson's mind: he did not write plays which people ought to like; he wrote plays they did like.[5] And so, I think, Shakespeare never, after *The Two Gentlemen*, used the love-friendship theme as a basis of serious plot action.[6] It was

4. *The Poetical Works of Edmund Spenser*, p. 423.

5. Professor Gerald Eades Bentley gave a most valuable comparison of the two dramatists in his Inaugural Lecture (March 15, 1946), "The Swan of Avon and the Bricklayer of Westminster," which has recently been issued in pamphlet form by Princeton University.

6. An exception is *The Two Noble Kinsmen* but it may be said that this play, based as it is on Chaucer's "Knight's Tale," is written in the new mode of tragicomedy.

not only unreal; it was stale and unprofitable. Of course the idea does re-appear, as for example, in the relationship between Antonio and Bas-sanio, but there is no conflict; the bond is not forfeit because of Bassa-nio's love for Portia. The simple fact is that certain argosies are wrecked or fail to arrive. Similar suggestions are twice found in *Much Ado,* but they are not developed. At one point Claudio thinks Pedro woos for him-self and sighs:

> Friendship is constant in all other things
> Save in the office and affairs of love: . . .[7]

In a moment Pedro tells the young man that the marriage is arranged, and we recognize Claudio's lament for the sheer conventional allusion that it was. So too it is with Beatrice's injunction to Benedick, "Kill Claudio." The instantaneous reaction is "Ha! Not for the world." And Benedick is not put to the test, for no sooner has he attempted to chal-lenge Claudio than Don John's trickery is made known. Now there is no thought of vengeance, for Claudio was not to blame. In both cases Shakespeare avoids the serious action which would result from a con-flict between love and friendship by immediately bringing on a scene which precludes any development. As Claudio learns that his lord has been faithful, so Benedick learns of the villainy of Don John. Cer-tainly the theme is used, but it is used for what it is—a conventional tag.

The second and more important reason for altering the substance of the plot will be found in the characters and relationship of Claudio and Hero. They have an integral function in the plot and purpose of the play which would be obscured were their affairs entangled with such tangen-tial ideas as a friendly rival would introduce. Hero must stand on her own as Claudio's prospective wife; she must not be the object for which two men strive, as she is in all the sources. As has been suggested, there is a definite reason for Shakespeare's presenting Hero and Claudio as he does, but since the evidence is connected with the general topic of the alteration of character, we must postpone this aspect of the inquiry for a short time.

The first result of Shakespeare's alteration of plot is the creation of a new character, Don John, who is, in his own words, a "plain-dealing vil-lain." The fact that there is an unmotivated protagonist of evil in Spen-ser's story of Phedon and Claribell has been a temptation to regard this character as the prototype, in fact the immediate original of Don John.[8]

7. II, i, 182–183. Here and throughout I quote from my edition of the play (F. S. Crofts [New York, 1948]), but for ease of reference I give the act, scene, and line of the passages as they appear in Professor Kittredge's *The Complete Works of Shake-speare.*

8. Alwin Thaler, "Spenser and *Much Ado About Nothing*," *Studies in Philology,* XXXVII (1940), 225–235.

In first discussing this brief narrative interlude from *The Faerie Queene,* I suggested that Spenser was adapting from Ariosto for a particular purpose, namely the exemplification of the sin of rage or irrational anger : Phedon proceeds from one murder to another since he is a victim of such a passion. When first seen by Guyon, Phedon is in the power of Furor who is being urged on by Occasion. If we transfer these allegorical figures to the exemplum, Phedon becomes Furor and Philemon, Occasion. Had Spenser preserved the Ariosto source intact with Philemon in love with Claribell, the very nature of Occasion would have been altered, and the application of the exemplum would have been confused. In somewhat the same fashion Spenser alters events by means of Claribell's death and Pryene's confession. The purpose of these changes is plain : Spenser adapts the plot for use as an exemplum which will immediately clarify his newly introduced allegorical figures. His imitation makes these alterations to suit his purpose. There is no comparison of this purpose and Shakespeare's, and there is no reason to refuse Shakespeare the same freedom in imitation that we are forced by the facts of the matter to allow Spenser.

In *Much Ado* Don John is a perpetrator of evil and the deception is evil. It is not the device of a rival, nor does Shakespeare intend it to be anything other than it is. This is the attitude which is found in the Ariosto versions where Polynesso is a scheming villain, a Machiavel ready for any deceit or forswearing to achieve his ends. Why he is such a person, why he acts as he does is not a matter to be explained or analyzed. Such a character is a most necessary part of the plot if we will remember the emphasis that the different adapters placed on the events. The deception is the chief plot device which makes this an interesting love story. In Bandello and Belleforest the actual execution is transferred from Girondo to a young courtier employed for the purpose, and he is the villain because only a villain could carry out such a plot. It should be recalled in this connection that Belleforest makes much of this young man whom Bandello was content to describe as "a young courtier, a man of slight intelligence, one to whom evil is more pleasing than good." These few words are expanded by the Frenchman into a paragraph defining a thorough-going Machiavel. Thus in all the sources and in Shakespeare the impulse is the same. An evil deed is the nexus of the plot and happen it must. The perpetrator must be a villain whose deeds an Elizabethan would never think of questioning.

In a way Don John is an adjunct of plot as is the duke in *Measure for Measure.* As Professor Lawrence remarks, the latter is a stage duke who is necessary to instigate and control events.[9] Although Don John has not been accorded the critical attention lavished on the duke, it is well to

9. William Witherle Lawrence, *Shakespeare's Problem Comedies* (New York, 1931), p. 102.

make his position clear, for the deception is an important part of the play, and it must be understood in the light of its sources and contemporary usage. In contrast with our world which searches out causes and motivations both in the criticism and creation of literature, the Renaissance willingly accepted the facts of a narrative. This does not mean that probability was altogether disregarded, though a reading of such fiction as the Peninsular Romance might conclude with this view; rather it means that given a situation the author worked within the scheme of things which this imposed. In tragedy Shakespeare is not so much interested in why Cordelia refuses to accept her father's caprice as in assessing the significance of what happens as a result of Lear's action. Hamlet may lament his mother's hasty remarriage but the reasons for Gertrude's conduct are not part of the play. So in comedy we are given none but the most casual reasons for Viola's decision to assume man's attire and seek service with Orsino. Without any immediate causation Duke Frederick decides that Rosalind is a threat to his security, and so she is banished. Citation of such unexplained incidents could be continued indefinitely but there is no need to enforce the obvious. The events are established and, though they may be modified, those happenings which are a part of the essential plot structure are accepted. Neither Shakespeare nor his audience was moved by psychological considerations to voice an "Everlasting Why." No more, in fact, were Aeschylus and the Athenians. Their interest, unlike our vitiated own, sought to understand and make comprehensible that which had occurred. Here again imitation does not deny originality, as we shall see when we realize how nicely the deception suits Shakespeare's view of the relationship of Claudio and Hero. Accepting the basic facts, Shakespeare alters them but does not lose the novelty and complication inherent in the plot against Hero. Thus Don John fits into the play as a very necessary agent. That he is a Machiavel, a popular stage villain, adds to the popular appeal, but he is not here primarily as a concession to the groundlings.

Following the transference to Don John of the role of instigator, the playwright is faced with a difficulty that is peculiar to the stage. First of all he must plan some means whereby Claudio and the others may learn that Hero has been falsely accused. Secondly, whatever device is used for this must also make it possible for the audience to know *before* the denunciation scene that the truth is out and that all will be put right. Otherwise the denunciation will be viewed as a most serious and tragic event. With foreknowledge the audience may be touched emotionally, but they will also realize the pathetic irony of Claudio's harshness and Hero's gentle defense. Neither of these demands was made upon the previous authors, who had a rival to confess or a rescued maid to tell her sad story. Nor were these authors in any trouble with their readers as to the outcome. We expect that Rinaldo will arrive in the nick of time to rescue

Genevra, and we know from the prefatory material that Timbreo will make Fenicia his wife. Even in the Italian plays, *Gli duoi fratelli rivali* and *Il Fedele,* and in the English and Latin versions of the latter, there is no problem such as Shakespeare faced in *Much Ado.* The very nature of the "commedia erudita" helped, for with complication piled on complication there is only one way out—a grand denouement wherein everybody is kept quite busy explaining the twisted threads to one another and the audience.

Shakespeare's skill in plot construction needed no such obvious device as this, since he created the characters fitting for his purpose. The villains are caught by the Watch before the hour appointed for the wedding, and there is a twofold reaction on the part of the audience. First and most obvious is a feeling of relief because the truth is known, but coupled with this is a feeling of suspense. Will the news get through in time? In a sense the situation is similar to the old reliable formula of the films where the camera flashes back and forth between the wagon train surrounded by savage redskins and the troop of cavalry charging to the rescue. But where we might expect the thundering hoofbeats, we have the slow and deliberate footsteps of the redoubtable Dogberry. Only such a watch could have dimly perceived the villainy afoot, and only such witless wits as Dogberry and Verges could have hampered the immediate revelation of that villainy. And Shakespeare makes the most of this situation. Until the closing lines of Act III it is still possible for Leonato to learn of Borachio's knavery; but ironically enough Leonato is so impatient of the bumbling buffoons before him, so anxious to speed his daughter's marriage, that he cannot take time to discover the one fact that would make the marriage possible. Such complete integration of character and plot moving to a height of suspense is either a most fortuitous combination of accidents or else it is the result of deliberate planning by a skilled theatrical craftsman. In view of the fact that there is no trace of either the characters or the element of suspense in the sources, the latter conclusion seems the correct one.

CLAUDIO AND HERO

Alteration of plot demands, as we have seen, certain new characters and Don John's henchmen, Conrade and Borachio, play their small parts as adjuncts of their master. But of somewhat more importance than such new characters are those who are altered and those who are added because of the completely new subplot of the deception of Benedick and Beatrice. At first glance there seems to be no connection between the two plots except for the appearance of Hero and Claudio as agents in the tricking of Benedick and Beatrice, and it has been this seeming lack of integration which has been considered a weakness of the play or has led

to the suggestion that the quarreling lovers were put in to liven up a
rather somber story. If we keep in mind the careful manipulation of plot
which has been demonstrated in connection with Dogberry, it should be
reasonable to assume that there is some design in the rest of the play. One
may object that if there were any such design it should be apparent and
should have been noted long ago. As a general premise such an objection
is not one to be tossed aside lightly, but in this case there does seem to be
an acceptable explanation. Briefly, the reason why the design has not
been perceived is that the true nature of Claudio and Hero and their relationship has been misunderstood. Perhaps the truth might be gleaned
from a careful reading of the play, but the reader would need to be well
versed in the marriage ways of the Elizabethans and well endowed with
critical perception. Certainly many who have written about the play have
had the requisite knowledge, but they have been misled by their own
inclination to identify Hero and Claudio as romantic literary lovers. Such
a view is perhaps understandable. Benedick, for example, talks as though
Claudio were a conventional lover and endows him with speeches and
behavior which the audience never hears or sees. But such tirades are a
part of Benedick's humor as an enemy of love and are not necessarily true.
A comparison of both Hero and Claudio with their prototypes in the
sources will show that these two are not fashioned from the usual literary
pattern.

   In all those versions wherein the lovers are given any extensive treatment, the hero is a conventionalized lover. Timbreo walks before Fenicia's house to gaze upon her beauty and feed the fire of love. He sends
letters and embassies. As we have seen, Belleforest develops the character still further, describing the inception of love through the familiar figure of beauty's blaze entering the eye and traveling to the heart. We are
given the full text of a typical love letter and that of a love poem. The
entire subject is argued in wearisome detail by Fénicie and her nurse.
With Beverley and Whetstone the lovers become the archetypes of conventional Renaissance lovers. Their love sickness is of a unity with that
suffered by numberless victims of Cupid's arrow from the *Songes and
Sonettes* through the poetry and fiction of the century. Their secret messages, their clandestine meetings, their happiness, their sorrows, their
reconciliation, their love language, the tropes, which describe them are in
themselves echoes and are in turn echoed in countless other tales of romantic love. Orlando is of the same pattern, even though he does not
measure up to Rosalind's high standard of the necessary marks of a lover.

A lean cheek, which you have not; a blue eye and sunken, which you have
not; an unquestionable spirit, which you have not; a beard neglected, which
you have not. But I pardon you for that, for simply your having in beard is

a younger brother's revenue. Then your hose should be ungarter'd, your bonnet unbanded, your sleeve unbutton'd, your shoe untied, and everything about you demonstrating a careless desolation.[10]

Nevertheless Orlando does very well. He mars the bark of trees by scratching out love songs on them; he adorns other trees with manuscripts of very bad poetry; he loves so that "neither rhyme nor reason can express how much," and he has no desire to be cured of his passion. Of a somewhat more mature nature is Orsino, but he too is a lover who lyrically apostrophizes the "Spirit of Love" and sadly puns on Curio's simple phrase, "The hart."

Of such simples was a good Elizabethan literary lover compounded, but Claudio, the favorite of Don Pedro, is made of other stuff. Unlike Ariodant who, overcome by the thought of Genevra's falseness, seeks only solitude and death, Claudio seeks the most cruel vengeance in a public defamation of his bride-to-be before the very altar where they were to be married. Timbreo sought no such vengeance; he sent word by an intermediary telling what he had seen and advising Fenecia to marry her lover, for he (Timbreo) would have no further dealings with her. Ariodant was so faithful a lover that in spite of his belief in Genevra's dishonesty, he returned to fight against his own brother in her behalf. Claudio, on the other hand, refrains from a duel with the aggrieved Leonato because of his soldierly scruples about fighting a less worthy and unequal adversary. The only suggestion of sympathy for the sorrowing family is that briefly expressed by Pedro. This same callousness is intensified when, following the departure of Leonato and his brother, Benedick appears. He is greeted with joy because Claudio and the duke wish to jest with him.

Thus it is easy to understand why there is general critical agreement in regarding Claudio as an unpleasant young man who behaves very badly. According to the standards of romantic love Claudio deserves the title of "cad" or "bounder," but unfortunately for those who wish to hurl opprobrium upon him, the plain fact is that Claudio is not a romantic lover and cannot therefore be judged by the artificial standards of literary convention. For example, how does Claudio fall in love? He tells Pedro

> O my lord,
> When you went onward on this ended action,
> I looked upon her with a soldier's eye,
> That liked, but had a rougher task in hand
> Than to drive liking to the name of love;
> But now I am returned, and that war-thoughts
> Have left their places vacant, in their rooms
> Come thronging soft and delicate desires,

10. *As You Like It*, III, ii, 392–403.

All prompting me how fair young Hero is,
Saying I liked her ere I went to wars.[11]

The verb describing the young man's feeling is significantly "like" not "love." Indeed, in his own words Claudio differentiates between "liking" and "the name of love." Cupid's dart has not struck Claudio, nor has the blaze of beauty ignited the usual furious flames.

The first indication of his interest in Hero is a question to Benedick directly the company have departed and left these two alone in the first scene of the play.

CLAUDIO   Benedick, didst thou note the daughter of Signior Leonato?
BENEDICK   I noted her not, but I looked on her.
CLAUDIO   Is she not a modest young lady? [12]

Benedick, refusing a straight answer, is importuned: "No, I pray thee speak in sober judgment"; and "Thou thinkest I am in sport. I pray thee tell me truly how thou likest her." [13] Neither Orlando nor Romeo asks other people what they think of Rosalind or Juliet; these lovers know that they have fallen desperately in love. Orlando is struck dumb and cannot even say "I thank you" to "heavenly Rosalind" who has given him the chain from about her neck. Romeo is more loquacious; indeed, his first vision of Juliet is followed almost at once by

> O, she doth teach the torches to burn bright!
> It seems she hangs upon the cheek of night
> Like a rich jewel in an Ethiop's ear—
> Beauty too rich for use, for earth too dear!
> So shows a snowy dove trooping with crows
> As yonder lady o'er her fellows shows.
> The measure done, I'll watch her place of stand
> And, touching hers, make blessed my rude hand.
> Did my heart love till now? Forswear it, sight!
> For I ne'er saw true beauty till this night.[14]

Whatever may be our view of Claudio, it is certain that he is no lover in the sense that these two are. Moreover he is not impetuous. Benedick reveals the secret to Pedro:

BENEDICK   . . . he is in love. With who? Now that is your Grace's part. Mark how short his answer is: with Hero, Leonato's short daughter.

11. *Much Ado*, I, i, 298–307. Of this passage Hazlitt (*Characters of Shakespear's Plays* [London, 1884], p. 210) observed that it was "as pleasing an image of the entrance of love into a youthful bosom as can well be imagined." Similar differentiation between "love" and "like" is found in Sidney's sonnet, "Not at the first sight, nor with a dribbled shot" (Hebel and Hudson, *Poetry of the English Renaissance* [New York, 1938], p. 106), where is found the line, "I saw and liked; I liked but loved not."

12. *Much Ado*, I, i, 164–166.

13. *Ibid.*, I, i, 171, 180.

14. *Romeo and Juliet*, I, v, 46–55. Compare this with Claudio's use of a jewel figure, *Much Ado*, I, i, 181–182.

CLAUDIO   If this were so, so were it uttered.
BENEDICK   Like the old tale, my lord: "It is not so, nor 'twas not so;
but indeed, God forbid it should be so."
CLAUDIO   If my passion change not shortly, God forbid it should be
otherwise.
PEDRO   Amen, if you love her; for the lady is very well worthy.
CLAUDIO   You speak this to fetch me in, my lord.[15]

It is perhaps unnecessary to point out that romantic lovers do not think or
speak of being "fetched in," nor does it ever enter their minds that their
passions may change. This cautious streak in Claudio is still evident
when, at the conclusion of his private talk with his patron, he remarks,

> But lest my liking might too sudden seem,
> I would have salved it with a longer treatise.[16]

Naturally he is cautious. As a young favorite of the duke contemplat-
ing matrimony he has many things to think on, if he is to make a proper
alliance. As soon as Benedick leaves them, Claudio opens a serious discussion with Pedro. "My liege, your Highness now may do me good." [17]
In other words, he seeks Pedro's assistance in the marriage, but first
there is a most important point that needs to be ascertained before
Claudio asks the prince to proceed in his behalf. Unlike Romeo or Orlando, Claudio is a careful suitor with an interest in finances; he inquires,
"Hath Leonato any son, my lord?" Don Pedro, also a realist, readily
understands, as his answer demonstrates, "No child but Hero; she's his
only heir." [18] To this is appended the query, "Dost thou affect her,
Claudio?" Pedro does not talk of love, for this is not a love match in the
romantic sense. Obviously Claudio likes the girl, as he then proceeds to
explain in the lines quoted above and that is all to the good; but what
Claudio is really interested in is a good and suitable marriage.

The propriety of the match as Shakespeare presents it is in contrast
with the situation in the earlier versions. Shakespeare's Leonato is gov-
ernor of Messina; not so in Bandello and Belleforest, where the inferior
social position of the heroine is advanced as the real reason for Timbreo's
letter of rejection. Claudio's social position is, of course, identical with
that of Timbreo but is unlike that of Ariodant who is but a knight aspir-
ing for the daughter of a king.[19] Again Shakespeare has altered, and the

15. *Much Ado*, I, i, 214–225.
16. *Ibid.*, I, i, 316–317.
17. *Ibid.*, I, i, 292.
18. *Ibid.*, I, i, 296–299. In describing his feigned niece to the repentant Claudio, Leonato (V, i, 297–299) stresses this same point as a recommendation for this new bride:
> My brother hath a daughter,
> Almost the copy of my child that's dead,
> And she alone is heir to both of us.

19. Whereas Beverley has both lovers reflect on the disparity of their social positions
as a possible impediment, Sir John Harington finds a *"good morall obseruation"* in *"the*

changes have a definite part in his scheme of things. The elevation of
Leonato from the status of mere gentleman to the governorship of Messina has not, I think, been noted as a fact of any importance or significance, but when a favorite of the prince decides to marry he must not
choose beneath his station. Margaret of Fressingfield may by sheer virtue ascend from her rustic dairy to share the eminence of her husband,
the earl of Lincoln; but in the real world such marriages were honored
more in the breach than the observance.

Although deception is one of the themes of his play, Shakespeare did
not try to deceive his audience into thinking that Claudio was a romantic
lover. The pattern was clear enough, and if the words of the young man
were not enough, the matter was further clarified when the prince offered to act in Claudio's behalf. For a later age, particularly one devoted
to the premise that true love conquers all, levels all barriers, leads to
joyous matrimony and wedded bliss, the facts that have been adduced
have little meaning. But such an age should remember that William
Shakespeare himself gave evidence in the legal proceedings instituted by
Stephen Belott against his father-in-law, Christopher Mountjoy, who
had broken his promise to give a marriage portion of £60 and to make a
will leaving £200 to his daughter, Belott's wife. Shakespeare was called
upon not only because he had been living in Mountjoy's house at the
time when the apprentice married his master's daughter but because he
helped to arrange the marriage. Urged on by Mistress Mountjoy, Shakespeare persuaded Belott to the fatal step.[20]

Nor should we forget George Chapman's part in the complicated mari-
tal affairs of Agnes Howe, the young heiress. Thanks to Professor Sisson's discoveries [21] we now know that this eminent dramatist abandoned
his usual vein and turned to the writing of a domestic drama dealing with
the machinations of John Howe to arrange for his daughter a marriage
that would be profitable to him. Three principal suitors were betrothed
to the girl and from them, and a number of others, the father profited as
best he could. Professor Sisson's reconstruction of this lost play, *The Old
Joiner of Aldgate,* gives us a realistic account of a most complicated
mariage de convenance.

But we should not conclude that the custom was limited to London
tradesmen such as Mountjoy and Howe; in all classes of society love was
a very minor consideration in arranging marriages. For example, Mr.

---

choise of Geneura, *who being a great Ladie by birth, yet chose rather a gallant faire
conditioned gentleman then a great Duke"* (*Orlando Furioso,* p. 39). To an Elizabethan
the question of social position was a very real consideration in marriage.

20. The depositions from the Court of Requests proceeding Bellot *vs.* Mountjoy were
first printed by C. W. Wallace, *Shakespeare and His London Associates, Nebraska University Studies,* Vol. X (1910). The relevant material is easily available in Sir Edmund
Chambers, *William Shakespeare* (2 vols., Oxford, 1930), II, 90–95.

21. C. J. Sisson, "*The Old Joiner of Aldgate* by Chapman," *Lost Plays of Shakespeare's Age* (Cambridge, 1936), pp. 12–79.

John Stanhope of Harrington in a letter to Sir Christopher Hatton discusses marriage plans for his daughter:

. . . after two or three days' rest, I took my daughter with me to my brother's house; where leaving her, I came to Carlisle to finish in some sort or other with my Lord Scrope our former agreement touching the marriage of our children, whom I find, as ever, so still desirous to proceed according to our first intent; and therefore have agreed to meet his Lordship again a month hence, in a progress which he intendeth into Lancashire, where the young couples may see one another, and after a little acquaintance, may resolve accordingly.[22]

Here we see two Elizabethan fathers arranging a proper marriage for their children who have not as yet seen one another. Claudio has at least seen Hero, but he has not spoken with her or even written her a letter. A very proper young man, he is proceeding through the proper channels. Obviously he must have the prince's permission, and if he is fortunate the prince may act in his behalf, or, as he says, "My liege, your Highness now may do me good." This then explains why Shakespeare has Pedro tell Hero of Claudio's affection and arrange the marriage with Leonato.

In Bandello and Belleforest, Timbreo employs a friend to make the necessary arrangements, as is quite proper; but Shakespeare, by transferring this office to Pedro, puts the marriage on quite another basis. Now the alliance is one blessed by royal authority, and Hero's alleged misconduct becomes a very serious matter of which Don John makes the most that he may. When he appears to make the accusation against Hero, the villain addresses himself to his brother because of the prince's share in arranging the match. Claudio may hear what is to be said since it concerns him, and Don John continues: "You may think I love you not; let that appear hereafter, and aim better at me by that I now will manifest. For my brother (I think he holds you well and in dearness of heart) hath holpe to effect your ensuing marriage: surely suit ill spent and labor ill bestowed." [23] Offered proof of the charge both Claudio and Pedro are prepared for violent action. The former resolves "in the congregation where I should wed, there will I shame her," [24] while the prince, recognizing his responsibility, says, "And as I wooed for thee to obtain her, I will join with thee to disgrace her." [25] And later Pedro's bitter words reveal his revulsion and the blow to his own pride:

> What should I speak?
> I stand dishonored that have gone about
> To link my dear friend to a common stale.[26]

22. Sir Harris Nicolas, *Memoirs of the Life and Times of Sir Christopher Hatton* (London, 1847), p. 78.
23. *Much Ado*, III, ii, 97–103.
24. *Ibid.*, III, ii, 127–129.
25. *Ibid.*, III, ii, 129–130.
26. *Ibid.*, IV, i, 64–66.

Viewed as a mariage de convenance the projected alliance and its breach demand another standard of judgment than that of romantic love. The public denunciation of Hero is an unpleasant affair, but Pedro and Claudio are more than justified, since they accept for truth the evidence which they have seen. Claudio likes Hero in the same way that Mr. Stanhope and Lord Scrope hoped their children would like one another, but Claudio is not madly in love with his bride-to-be. He has hoped for, and the prince has arranged, a suitable match. If Hero has a clandestine lover she has affronted all the proprieties. Unchastity is but one of her sins, the others being a deliberate flaunting of the arrangements of her father and Pedro and an attempt to pass herself off to her proud young husband as undamaged merchandise. In the eyes of the aggrieved she was not only a wanton but an intentional perpetrator of fraud.

Even the most cursory examination of the available evidence emphasizes the businesslike attitude toward marriage in Shakespeare's England. In the proceedings of the Court of Requests, for example, is listed a variety of cases concerning every aspect of marriage arrangements. To cite but a few, these cases comprise a "Reward for bringing about a marriage," "Gifts promised for negotiating a marriage," "Expenses of courting defendant's niece, the engagement being broken off," " 'Gifts and benefits' promised by defendants on plaintiff's marriage with their daughter," "Lands . . . comprised in a marriage settlement," "Breach of promise of marriage," and "Money delivered to second defendant under promise of marrying plaintiff." [27] While the poets sang of love, the real world went about its business of dealing practically with the divine passion. A rejected suitor with a literary flair bemoaned his loss in appropriate verse; his less talented and more forthright brother hied himself to the courts and sued for the "Recovery of gloves, rings, and other presents, made in anticipation of a marriage which was broken off." [28]

The chief thing that could affect contracted marriages, aside from occasional insubordination, was a doubt of legality or any indication of fraud, and there were suits for "Money paid in respect of a marriage which proved illegal." [29] Since business was business, it was, understandably enough, to the interest of fathers and go-betweens to keep a sharp eye out for "pretended" or secret marriages. A secret marriage, therefore, between the earl of Leicester and Lettice, countess of Essex, most emphatically did not satisfy the bride's father. He knew too well the nature of his new son-in-law to be content with anything save a public ceremony which he could witness, and such a second wedding was celebrated.[30]

27. In the order given the relevant cases are Court of Requests: XXX/43; XCVII/5; CIX/38; LXXVIII/104; XLIV/19; XXXI/37; CXV/3.
28. Requests, LXV/55.
29. Requests, XCIV/23.
30. William Camden, *The History of . . . Elizabeth* (London, 1675), pp. 217–218.

Against such a background the businesslike, callous, and even venge-
ful spirit of both Claudio and Don Pedro becomes understandable. A
suitable marriage having been arranged, it now seems to them that Hero
would trick them if she could, and so her death is not a matter of regret
but an instance of wickedness receiving its just reward. They are, of
course, repentant when Hero is exonerated, and Claudio is willing to do
any penance which Leonato may impose. Even here the new marriage is
presented in the same light as the old, for Leonato asks that Claudio
marry his brother's daughter and "give her the right you should have
given her cousin." [31] The right is, of course, a suitable husband, but there
are the usual considerations. The new bride is described by Leonato as
"almost the copy of my child that's dead," and he adds, significantly,
"and she alone is heir to both of us." [32] Claudio's penance is both light
and well paid.

It will be remembered that just such a general tone of Realpolitik was
evident in Bandello. Shakespeare does not make Claudio the straight-
forward sensualist that was Timbreo, nor does he make Leonato a saga-
cious father trying to assure his daughter of some or any marriage, even
though she must hide in the country for a couple of years so as to deceive
potential suitors. Rather the realism of the matter is shown by Shakespeare in the essential mariage de convenance situation. Of this there is no
hint in Bandello or in any of the other versions. In Bandello Timbreo is a
frank sensualist forced into marriage by his desires. Elsewhere the hero
is purely conventional, a romantic lover. Actually such alteration does
not require any change in the character of the heroine as she appears in
Bandello and Belleforest. Here she is the well-brought-up young girl, the
dutiful daughter who knows what deceivers men are and how to behave
herself. On the other hand, the heroine in the Ariosto descent is quite a
different character. She is impetuous, romantic, and wilful, and Hero
does represent a great alteration from such a pattern. Since Shakespeare
has changed the fundamental relationship from one of convention to a
reality, it seems fruitless to attempt any direct explanation of Hero's
origins. She is what she is because of the situation in which she plays a
principal part.

The influence of this last fact is easily demonstrable. Whereas Fenicia
rejects all letters, messages, gifts, and embassies, Hero is not faced with
such trials which are necessary temptations for Fenicia whose suitor is
the ardent Don Timbreo; but Claudio, the soul of propriety, will make
no such furtive assaults on Hero's virtue. Similarly there is no need for
Hero to discuss her suitor as does Belleforest's heroine. Fénicie, in tire-
some paragraphs, is forced to expound the whole duty of a virtuous
daughter, but this she does as a specific reaction to the immoral sugges-

31. *Much Ado*, V, i, 300.
32. *Ibid.*, V, i, 297-298.

tions of her nurse. Hero, not being wooed by such a lover and fortunately being without the attendance of such a confidante, has no need to orate. She is involved in quite a different situation: a mariage de convenance wherein she is very simply the dutiful daughter. Unlike Juliet who already has a husband and cannot marry Paris, Hero, perfectly content with her father's choice, does not object to the match, with the result that there is no conflict, no action except that which arises from the deception.

This lack of action clarifies many things, chief among them, Hero's taciturnity. She has remarkably few lines except those connected with the Benedick-Beatrice plot. During the whole first act, although she is on stage for a considerable time, she has but one line, a mere tag, "My cousin means Signior Benedick of Padua." [33] She is equally reticent during and after her betrothal. Leonato announces the match, but it is Beatrice who speaks and her words are an admonishment: "Speak cousin; or if you cannot, stop his mouth with a kiss and let him not speak neither." [34] From this we may deduce a bit of stage business involving a maidenly offering of her lips; but the rest is silence, for no words pass those lips that we can hear, although Hero is supposed to be whispering words of love in Claudio's ear. Perhaps modesty may be the rein upon her tongue, but really there is no need for her to say anything. She has not hitherto talked with Claudio nor has she been wooed by him. As Beatrice remarks, "It is my cousin's duty to make curtsy and say, 'Father, as it please you'; but yet for all that, cousin, let him be a handsome fellow, or else make another curtsy and say, 'Father, as it please me.'" [35] Presumably Claudio is a handsome fellow, and Hero does her duty, but it were the height of folly to imagine her passionately in love as was Juliet. She makes but one reference to her bridegroom on the morning of her wedding when she casually observes, "These gloves the Count sent me, they are an excellent perfume." [36] Maidenly reticence can hardly be offered as an excuse for Hero's failure to talk about her future husband. The conversation which precedes her glove reference is neither maidenly nor modest. No, the plain fact of the matter is that Hero is not emotionally involved; she is an obedient and dutiful daughter, just such a daughter as old Capulet and many another Renaissance father would have wished to have.

Such a character is not too frequent a performer on the stage because, as we have noted, there can arise no action from such passiveness. However, there is an excellent and more loquacious member of the genre in *Eastward Ho*. Mildred, the dutiful daughter of the goldsmith Touchstone, is presented as a contrast to her willful and socially ambitious sister

33. *Ibid.*, I, i, 36.
34. *Ibid.*, II, i, 321–323.
35. *Ibid.*, II, i, 55–59.
36. *Ibid.*, III, iv, 62–63.

Gertrude who scorns their father's counsel and marries the bankrupt Sir Petronel Flash. Without any warning Touchstone announces to Mildred that she is to marry his apprentice, Golding. In words that certainly warmed the heart of every father in the audience, she replies: "Sir, I am all yours; your body gave me life; your care and love, happiness of life; let your virtue still direct it, for to your wisdom I wholly dispose myself." [37] As is to be expected, happiness and prosperity are the lot of Mildred and Golding; ruin and disaster the just reward of proud Gertrude and her mountebank knight. Very little is said about Mildred, for there is nothing dramatic in her situation; the main action focuses on Gertrude and Petronel.

Similarly there is little or no action implicit in the affairs of Claudio and Hero, and were it not for the deception there could be no play. In the presentation of this one source of action Shakespeare has altered his original. Only in Ariosto and the versions derived from him is there a maid dressed in her mistress's robes, and there we have a very clear explanation of the disguise. There is no such clarity in *Much Ado*. Margaret's part in the plot is never explained. All we ever hear by way of explanation is Leonato's brief reference:

> But Margaret was in some fault for this,
> Although against her will, as it appears
> In the true course of all the question.[38]

More than this we do not know, and elsewhere there is the same uncertainty. Borachio, first broaching the scheme, advises Don John to tell the prince and Claudio that he (Borachio) is Hero's lover. In the same scene is found the ambiguous reference: ". . . hear me call Margaret Hero, hear Margaret term me Claudio . . ." [39] In all subsequent accounts of what happened the identity of the lover is unknown and there is no mention of the conversation between the false Hero and her paramour. The prince and Claudio are deceived by their eyes, not their ears, and Borachio's confession gives the same impression: ". . . how you were brought into the orchard and saw me court Margaret in Hero's garments . . ." [40] But it is such contradiction that leads Professor Dover Wilson to posit an earlier play carelessly revised by Shakespeare. Although such an explanation neatly settles the problem by avoiding it, there really seems to be no need to worry the matter too much. There is no logical explanation, as was pointed out by Lewis Carroll in a letter to Ellen Terry:

37. *The Comedies of George Chapman*, ed. Thomas Marc Parrott (London, 1914), p. 473, ll. 168-170.
38. V, iv, 4-6.
39. *Ibid.*, II, ii, 44-45.
40. *Ibid.*, V, i, 243-245.

But even if Hero might be supposed to be so distracted as not to remember where she had slept the night before, or even whether she had slept *anywhere,* surely *Beatrice* has her wits about her! And when an arrangement was made, by which she was to lose, for one night, her twelve-months' bedfellow, is it conceivable that she didn't know *where* Hero passed the night? Why didn't *she* reply:

> "But good my lord sweet Hero slept.not there:
> She had another chamber for the nonce.
> 'Twas sure some counterfeit that did present
> Her person at the window, aped her voice,
> Her mien, her manners, and hath thus deceived
> My good Lord Pedro and this company?"

With all these excellent materials for proving an "alibi" it is incomprehensible that no one should think of it. If only there had been a barrister present, to cross-examine Beatrice!

"Now, ma'am, attend to me, please, and speak up so that the jury can hear you. Where did you sleep last night? Where did Hero sleep? Will you swear that she slept in her own room? Will you swear that you do not know where she slept?" I feel inclined to quote old Mr. Weller and to say to Beatrice at the end of the play (only I'm afraid it isn't etiquette to speak across the footlights):

> "Oh, Samivel, Samivel, vy vornt there a halibi?" [41]

There can no more be a cross-examination of Beatrice than there can be a confession by Margaret. All that matters is that Claudio and Pedro think the accusation true and behave as they do in the Temple. The deception per se is not important in Shakespeare's play. The significance is the real matter of importance. Shakespeare is not interested in Margaret as a deceived Dalinda; nor is he concerned with the variety of things that happen to Claudio and Hero before they reach the port of matrimony. In other words, those aspects of the story which appealed to Ariosto, Bandello, and the others are not for Shakespeare; his purpose is quite alien to that of other tellers of this tale. From what we have seen of Claudio and Hero, the significance of the deception is apparent. This is not a love match in the conventional sense; it is a proper marriage which is wrecked as easily as it is arranged, when there is a hint of fraud. The reaction of both the prince and Claudio to Hero's death and their behavior to both Leonato and Benedick are explicable on no other grounds. It is as though Shakespeare were saying to us, "Here is the fashion in the real world where marriage is essentially a business arrangement." The literary ideal and the reality are at variance, or as Rosalind observes: "Men have died from time to time, and worms have eaten them, but not for love." [42]

It may be that, according to modern standards, Shakespeare should have so plotted his play that there could be a ready and easy explanation

---

41. Quoted by Ellen Terry in *The Story of My Life* (London, 1908), p. 358.
42. *As You Like It,* IV, i, 106–108.

for Margaret's complicity and her silence, but again I would suggest that neither Shakespeare nor his audience bothered about motivation and logical explanation in the sense that we do. After all, the scene does take place off stage and is reported with a dearth of detail. It is not the subtle trick of a Polynesso; it is merely the source of the only action that can arise in the Hero-Claudio plot. As such it happens, and that is all we need be concerned with. There is no rival; Hero's affections are not engaged; action results from an external event. Viewed as a most necessary cog in the plot the deception should perhaps be acted out and not reported; but aside from the difficulty of representing the disguised Margaret, the reporting is not a fault, for it emphasizes the fact that the scene is external—a mere device which the dramatist uses but does not consider important for its own sake.

Although we have been concerned with the realism of the Hero-Claudio plot, we should not conclude that *Much Ado* is a satiric or problem comedy. It has been necessary to emphasize the realism of this plot because a failure to do has confused Shakespeare's intent. There is a real difference between the nonserious presentation of a realistic situation and the serious presentation of the same thing, and this play, unlike *Measure for Measure* or *All's Well,* is certainly not to be taken as a serious portrayal of unpleasant realism. If we think for a moment of the changes that are rung on the theme of deception, we will realize that the comic spirit has the upper hand. At the end of the opening scene Pedro decides to make use of the night's masking to hide his identity and, pretending to be Claudio, to woo Hero. The next two scenes are concerned with nothing but the overhearing of this. Antonio reports an incorrect version to his brother Leonato, while Borachio has the correct story for Don John. The first scene of Act II has yet more deceiving. Benedick, hiding his identity under a mask, must bear in silence a tongue-lashing from Beatrice. Claudio, pretending to be Benedick, receives from Don John the unpleasant and false information that the prince intends to marry Hero. No sooner is this matter set right and the betrothal of Claudio and Hero performed than Pedro plots the deception of Benedick and Beatrice. Even the Watch are part of the pattern, for they create out of their own misunderstanding that renowned thief "one Deformed." All this deceiving springs from but a single cause: various people are guilty of eavesdropping. Certainly the prince and Claudio are eavesdroppers when they secretly witness the false assignation, and both Benedick and Beatrice are brought to the altar by their sin of overhearing, or as Hero says:

> Of this matter
> Is little Cupid's crafty arrow made,
> That only wounds by hearsay.[43]

Of all this eavesdropping and deceiving there is no hint in the sources;

43. *Much Ado*, III, i, 21–23.

both are original with Shakespeare who uses the theme to achieve his comic purpose.

Thus has Shakespeare adapted the Hero-Claudio story to suit his non-serious treatment of it ; but this plot cannot stand by itself as comedy nor as a reflection of contemporary attitudes toward marriage. The comedy is made by Benedick and Beatrice whose love is another aspect of the nonromantic and whose marriage balances that of Claudio and Hero.

BENEDICK AND BEATRICE

As with Claudio and Hero, it is necessary to understand Benedick and Beatrice in contemporary terms if their place in the structure of the play is to be comprehended as part of an organic unity. Here in a strictly literal sense we abandon the sources, for no such characters are there to be found. A moment's reflection, however, may show us that a comparison of Shakespeare with his originals has led us to a point where something like the Benedick-Beatrice plot is an absolute necessity. With the Hero-Claudio affair a mariage de convenance whose only action is based on deception, there must be some sort of counterplot wherein deception is definitely comic. For such a contrast Benedick and Beatrice are admirably suited. But these two have a relevancy to the ideas of the play as well as to its plot. There is reason behind Shakespeare's creation of them, and this we may notice if we expand our study of sources to include previous literary appearances of such characters and the ideas which they propound.

Miss Mary Augusta Scott [44] pointed out certain parallels between Benedick and Beatrice on the one hand and Lord Gaspare Pallavicino and the Lady Emilia Pia on the other. The principal likenesses which Miss Scott observes are of a general nature. First, the Italian pair are witty and they speak in dramatic dialogue. Second, there is antagonism between them because Lord Gaspare is essentially antifeminist and as such is teased by the Lady Emilia who defends her sex. When it is suggested that the group define "a gentilwoman of the Palaice so facioned in all perfections, as these Lordes have facioned the perfect Courtier," [45] Lady Emilia expresses the pious hope that her adversary have no part in such a discussion, for he will surely fashion "one that can do nought elles but looke to the kitchin and spinn." [46] Resemblances of this sort there are between Castiglione and Shakespeare, but the frequency of the literary appearances of such characters throughout the century testifies to a widespread convention rather than to direct imitation.

It is likewise something of an oversimplification to regard, as does Mr.

44. *"The Book of the Courtyer:* A Possible Source of Benedick and Beatrice," PMLA, pp. 475–502.
45. *The Book of the Courtier,* ed. Walter Raleigh, p. 206.
46. *Ibid.*

D. L. Stevenson, Benedick and Beatrice as participants in the conventional "sex-duel," "quarreling over the nature of love." [47] Thus these two are viewed as a sort of culmination of "the amorous conflict" which began "in the poetry of Wyatt." [48] Such constant application of a thesis leads to an erroneous interpretation of the love relationship of Hero and Claudio and their function in the play, as well as to the questionable generalization that "Shakespeare's comedies of courtship . . . resolve a quarrel over the nature of love which had been current in English literature for about four centuries." [49] It is quite true that Benedick and Beatrice have perfectly obvious relations to the tradition of quarreling lovers, but an examination of what these two actually do and say precludes any attempt to make them sophisticated in the sense that the Lord Gaspare and the Lady Emilia are. Similarly there is a world of difference between Berowne and Rosaline, and Benedick and Beatrice, even though there are certain resemblances. The patterns of Elizabethan love behavior cannot be easily separated and analyzed according to strict definition.[50] Aside from this, the fact is that Benedick and Beatrice are characters in a play and their function within that framework limits and modifies so that they are something more than symbols of a convention.

Traditional elements are, in part, responsible for the dramatic popularity of Benedick and Beatrice, since the audience recognizes with pleasure that which is familiar, and there is exemplified in these two still another convention which has hitherto escaped notice, although a clue was offered when Miss Potts noted parallels between the persons of *Much Ado* and characters in *The Faerie Queene*.[51] Of these parallels, the late Professor Tucker Brooke remarked with characteristic irony, "Only a very clever person could have noted them, or could have left it, as Miss Potts does, to some strangely gifted reader to decide what they imply." [52] With an acute awareness of both possible and probable foolhardiness, I venture to suggest that at least one of the likenesses may be said to have apparent significance. There is a definite affinity between Beatrice and Mirabella, who is doomed by Cupid to a penance of two years' duration. She is mounted on "a mangy iade" led by "a lewd foole" and followed by another,

47. *The Love-Game Comedy*, p. 212.
48. *Ibid.*, p. 231.
49. *Ibid.*, p. 223.
50. Not only the work of Mr. C. S. Lewis on the various aspects of love in *The Faerie Queene* (*The Allegory of Love*), but the encyclopedic knowledge of the subject found in T. F. Crane's *Italian Social Customs of the Sixteenth Century* testify to the impossibility of any simple generalizations as to the nature of love behavior patterns. The whole subject is one needing thorough study.
51. Abbie Findlay Potts, "Spenserian 'Courtesy' and 'Temperance' in Shakespeare's *Much Ado About Nothing*," *Shakespeare Association Bulletin;* XVII (1942), 103–111, 126–133.
52. *The Year's Work in English Studies*, XXIII (1942), 110.

> . . . who hauing in his hand a whip,
> Her therewith yirks, and still when she complaines,
> The more he laughes, and does her closely quip,
> To see her sore lament, and bite her tender lip.[53]

The purpose of this unhappy wandering through the world is to afford Mirabella the opportunity to redeem herself by saving "so many loues, as she did lose." [54] For Mirabella the quest was difficult, since she had "through her dispiteous pride, whilest loue lackt place" destroyed some "two and twenty." [55] Though of mean parentage, the lady had "wondrous giftes of nature's grace"; [56] such beauty was hers that

> The beames whereof did kindle louely fire
> In th' harts of many a knight, and many a gentle squire.[57]

But to all her suitors Mirabella was indifferent, and the more she was praised "the more she did all loue despize," saying,

> She was borne free, not bound to any wight,
> And so would euer liue, and loue her owne delight.[58]

Arrogant in the power which her beauty gave her, she

> Did boast her beautie had such soueraine might,
> That with the onely twinckle of her eye,
> She could or saue, or spill, whom she would hight.
> What could the Gods doe more, but doe it more aright? [59]

Naturally such effrontery led to heavenly displeasure with the result that Mirabella was brought a captive unto the bar of Cupid's Court where she was examined and sentenced. Her guards on the journey are "Disdaine" who leads the horse and "Scorne" who scourges her.

These same two abstractions are used by Hero in describing her cousin:

> But Nature never framed a woman's heart
> Of prouder stuff than that of Beatrice.
> Disdain and Scorn ride sparkling in her eyes,
> Misprising what they look on, and her wit
> Values itself so highly that to her
> All matter else seems weak. She cannot love,

---

53. *The Poetical Works of Edmund Spenser*, p. 369. Hereafter references will be given to *The Faerie Queene* by Book, Canto, and stanza. The present citation is from VI, 7, 44.
54. *The Faerie Queene*, VI, 7, 37.
55. *Ibid.*, VI, 7, 38.
56. *Ibid.*, VI, 7, 28.
57. *Ibid.*
58. *Ibid.*, VI, 7, 30.
59. *Ibid.*, VI, 7, 31.

Nor take no shape nor project of affection,
She is so self-endeared.[60]

Hero's description seems to suit Mirabella quite as well as Beatrice; both misprise and both are self-endeared. Other comments on Beatrice confirm the resemblance. Benedick addresses her as "Lady Disdain." [61] When Pedro observes, "She cannot endure to hear tell of a husband," Leonato replies, "O, by no means. She mocks all her wooers out of suit." [62] This same theme of obduracy is mentioned again in the scene gulling Benedick; the prince feigns amazement at the news of Beatrice's love: "I would have thought her spirit had been invincible against all assaults of affection." [63]

There can be little doubt that these two ladies have a great deal in common, although there are equally obvious differences between them. But should we conclude that Shakespeare is imitating directly from Spenser or that both are imitating a common, nonexistent source? The simple answer seems to be that both are writing about the same object—the conventional "Disdainful Woman." Such a personage appears as a constant in the literature of the period. When, for example, Giletta wished to hide her love from Frizaldo, she adopted just such a conventional attitude. When Rinaldo, quite unaware of her dissembling, "saluted her by the name of his mystresse, very disdainfully and scornefully, or not at all she aunsweared him: On him shee frowned with a curst countenaunce." [64] Not only do the terms "disdain and scorn" appear, there is as well the adjective "curst" which Antonio applies with exactly the same significance. When Leonato advises Beatrice, "By my troth, niece, thou wilt never get thee a husband, if thou be so shrewd of thy tongue," Antonio adds, "In faith, she's too curst." [65] Here again there is no question of direct influence: both Whetstone and Shakespeare are using the well-established clichés in connection with a stereotype.[66] The pattern appears again and again. Colin Clout, like many another, loved a maiden who scorned him, and Rosalind, the widow's daughter of the glen, like Beatrice, Mirabella, and many another, fed her suitor with disdain. The Elizabethan Miscellanies abound with harsh descriptions of disdainful ladies, and the verses of such poets as Turbervile, Gascoigne, and Whetstone frequently upbraid the stony hearts which scorn them.

Although Beatrice may be reasonably classified as a "Disdainful Dame," she is not identical with Mirabella or any other woman we have

60. *Much Ado,* III, i, 49–56.
61. *Ibid.,* I, i, 119.
62. *Ibid.,* II, i, 362–365.
63. *Ibid.,* II, iii, 119–120.
64. *The Rocke of Regard,* p. 43.
65. *Much Ado,* II, i, 19–22.
66. Parallels between Beatrice and Katherine are of course obvious, but it is worth pointing out that the adjective "curst" is applied at least ten times to Katherine.

noted, and if we are to avoid the dangers of generalization, we must realize her composite nature. In point of fact Benedick's behavior is in some
ways closer to that of Mirabella. Whereas we have only the one slight
reference to Beatrice's mocking her suitors, Benedick himself boasts of
his cruelty to the sex: "But it is certain I am loved of all ladies, only you
excepted; and I would I could find in my heart that I had not a hard
heart, for truly I love none." [67] When Claudio asks his opinion of Hero,
our masculine Disdainer reveals the same attitude. "Do you question me
as an honest man should do, for my simple true judgment? or would you
have me speak after my custom, as being a professed tyrant to their
sex?" [68] This avowed custom of cruelty to women, while talked of, is
never demonstrated, for none of the many who love Benedick appears in
this play. Benedick, too, is really a composite of several conventions
brought to life by Shakespeare's genius. Generically he is a disdainer and
a quarreling lover, but certainly he is not to be equated with Berowne,
that eloquent defender of "the right Promethean fire," simply because he
engages in jesting with a woman for whom he finally admits love. The di-
versity of the character is pointed further by Miss Potts's notation of
parallels between him and Spenser's Braggadochio.[69] Beatrice, in the
opening scene, jests at his martial exploits; later Pedro observes, ". . .
in the managing of quarrels you may say he is wise, for either he avoids
them with great discretion, or undertakes them with a most Christianlike
fear." [70] Braggadochio exhibits the same characteristics, but again there
is no question of direct indebtedness; instead, Spenser and Shakespeare
are both using a familiar stereotype and in describing it they both use
familiar tropes.

Another familar idea which appears in *The Faerie Queene, The
Shepheardes Calendar,* and in other poetry and prose works helps to
explain the dramatic popularity of Benedick and Beatrice, as well as to
emphasize Shakespeare's use of ideas current in his own age which would
have an easy and definite appeal for his audience. Here again it is necessary to abandon sources in any strict sense, in favor of study which will
reveal something of the background of ideas and behavior patterns familiar to the dramatist and his audience. After the rescue of St. George
from the dungeons of Orgoglio, there is a brief interlude when, at Una's
request, Prince Arthur tells of his loves and lineage. In youth, the usual
time for love to burgeon, Prince Arthur avoided the infection because of
the good advice given him by old Timon.

67. *Much Ado,* I, i, 125-129.
68. *Ibid.,* I, i, 167-170.
69. "Spenserian 'Courtesy' and 'Temperance' in Shakespeare's *Much Ado About
Nothing,*" pp. 129-132.
70. *Much Ado,* II, iii, 197-200.

That idle name of loue, and louers life,
    As losse of time, and vertues enimy
    I euer scornd, and ioyd to stirre vp strife,
    In middest of their mournful Tragedy,
    Ay wont to laugh, when them I heard to cry,
    And blow the fire, which them to ashes brent . . .[71]

Such arrant defiance of Cupid can have but one result as the prince rue-fully admits:

    Nothing is sure, that growes on earthly ground:
    And who most trustes in arme of fleshly might,
    And boasts, in beauties chaine not to be bound,
    Doth soonest fall in disauentrous fight,
    And yeeldes his caytiue neck to victours most despight.[72]

The blind god has triumphed over the rebel

    Whose prouder vaunt that proud auenging boy
    Did soone pluck downe, and curbd my libertie.[73]

Equally defiant is Benedick as we are told by Beatrice who, learning that he has returned safely from the wars, defines him as rebel against Cupid. "He set up his bills here in Messina and challenged Cupid at the flight; and my uncle's fool, reading the challenge subscribed for Cupid and challenged him at the burbolt." [74] Later in the play when both Beatrice and Benedick have been deceived, Pedro refers to Benedick's opposition to the god of Love. "He hath twice or thrice cut Cupid's bowstring, and the little hangman dare not shoot at him." [75] The prince is here speaking in ironic vein because he and Claudio feel certain that they have succeeded in their deception, but the irony and humor are perfectly obvious to the audience for whom this aspect of Benedick's character has already been well established. The parallels with Prince Arthur may, however, be observed in further details. Benedick, like the prince, scorns "that idle name of love." When Claudio first asks an opinion on Hero, Benedick must at once attack conventional love language. "But speak you this with a sad brow? or do you play the flouting jack, to tell us Cupid is a good hare-finder, and Vulcan a rare carpenter?" [76] Similarly Benedick joys "to stirre up strife" for lovers. It is with evident pleasure that he teases Claudio with the quip, "the Prince hath got your Hero." [77]

71. *The Faerie Queene*, I, 9, 10.
72. *Ibid.*, I, 9, 11.
73. *Ibid.*, I, 9, 12.
74. *Much Ado*, I, i, 39–42.
75. *Ibid.*, III, ii, 10–12.
76. *Ibid.*, I, i, 184–187.
77. *Ibid.*, II, i, 199.

Using the willow, the conventional symbol of the forsaken lover, the disdainer exploits the situation to the full.

It is this use by Benedick of conventional literary love jargon in speaking with or about Claudio that has led to misunderstanding of this particular character. As we have observed, Claudio does not qualify as a romantic, even though Benedick talks as if he were, practically putting the clichés in his mouth. As Cupid's foe and a scorner of "the idle name of love," Benedick is always ready to ridicule the subject whether he has just cause or no. All he needs is the suggestion of fashionable love talk to send him into a tirade wherein he attacks such jargon. Claudio mentions his liking for Hero, and Benedick is off; Pedro observes that someday he will see Benedick look pale with love and the accused replies as we know he will. In just such a vein is Benedick's soliloquy which immediately precedes his deception. Ranting on at a great rate against love and Claudio as a lover, Benedick's words are wondrously ironic in view of what is to happen. Like Prince Arthur's, "his prouder vaunt that proud auenging boy [will] soone plucke downe." This is the stuff of comedy and should be understood in this as well as in its conventional sense.

It may, I think, be demonstrated that an Elizabethan audience would, early in the course of the play, realize what is going to happen to Benedick and Beatrice. As rebels against love their fate is sure and certain; they are destined to meet before the altar at the conclusion of the play. Whereas Mirabella is forced by Cupid to do penance, the usual rebel was treated as was Prince Arthur. Mirabella is punished because of her discourtesy and her story is therefore part of Book VI. The more usual pattern is exemplified by Arthur's fate. That Cupid's vengeance on the prince was in the familiar vein may be ascertained by reference to practically any of the poets of the time. In the March eclogue of *The Shepheardes Calendar*, Thomalin boasts how he discovered Cupid hiding in a bush and shot him with a burbolt. In revenge the god has shot him in the heel and now his wound festers sore. The preface to the eclogue makes it clear, though Thomalin's words are plain enough, that ". . . *in the person of Thomalin is meant some secrete freend, who scorned Loue and his knights so long, till at length him self was entangled, and vnwares wounded with the dart of some beautiful regard, which is Cupides arrowe.*" [78] Such is also the explanation advanced by Dan Bartholmew of Bathe for his unhappy love affair:

> I thinke the goddesse of revenge devysde,
> So to be wreackt on my rebelling will,
> Bycause I had in youthfull yeares dispysde,
> To taste the baytes, which tyste my fancie still.[79]

78. *The Poetical Works of Edmund Spenser*, p. 428.
79. *George Gascoigne's A Hundreth Sundrie Flowres*, ll. 49–52, p. 203.

There are constant references to this stereotype in practically all poets of the period. George Whetstone, for example, thus prefaces one set of his poems: "The contemptuous louer finding no grace where hee faithfully fauoreth, acknowledgeth his former scorne, vsed toward loue, to be the onely cause of his miseries." [80] Elsewhere Whetstone tells the sad story of "The hap, and hard fortune of a careless louer" who summoned by Cupid to yield to Beauty refused and was subsequently brought a captive to "Beauties barre." [81] A long and horrendous sentence is pronounced whereby the prisoner is forced to endure unrequited love.[82]

Although Benedick has been "an obstinate heretic in the despite of Beauty," [83] he is not condemned to suffer the pangs of unrequited love. Instead he is matched with another offender against the laws of love. A sentimental view may incline us to envision the married state of these two as one of unalloyed bliss, since "they really did love one another all the time." Be that as it may, the conclusion of the play shows the lovers, even in the midst of capitulation, still struggling to maintain the dignity of their former positions, and points, at the least, to a lively union. Benedick agrees to matrimony and seeks to gain the last word. "Come, I will have thee, but, by this hand, I take thee for pity." [84] Beatrice accepts, caustic as ever, "I would not deny you; but by this good day, I yield upon great persuasion, and partly to save your life, for I was told you were in a consumption," [85] and gets, momentarily, the last word. An Elizabethan audience would not, I think, have taken the sentimental view. Aware of the conventions and delighting in their perception of the situation and its inevitable result, they would take it for the wondrous comedy that it is.

The comedy, of course, arises from many elements, but always there is Shakespeare's hand at work blending conventions and creating character. Benedick and Beatrice are not merely rebels against love and its language; they are, as well, juxtaposed; so that their rebellion may find a tangible enemy in each other. Each represents to the other that which each scorns, and therein lie the complexity of their characters and the source of humor. Actually their rebellion is not to be taken too seriously. As we have seen, Benedick refers to his "custom, as being a professed tyrant to their sex," but at once he contrasts an opinion delivered on this basis with "my simple true judgment." [86] The assumed pose of this is

80. "The Garden of Vnthriftinesse," *The Rocke of Regard,* p. 100.
81. *Ibid.,* pp. 80–82.
82. This is a rather crude adaptation of one of Gascoigne's better poems, "Gascoignes araignement," which concludes,
    "Thus am I Beauties bounden thrall,
        At hir commaunde when she doth call,"
A Hundreth Sundrie Flowres, pp. 144–145.
83. *Much Ado,* I, i, 236–237.
84. *Ibid.,* V, iv, 92–93.
85. *Ibid.,* V, iv, 94–97.
86. *Ibid.,* I, i, 167–168.

consonant with Beatrice's "I was born to speak all mirth and no matter," or, "then there was a star danced, and under that was I born." [87] They both have light hearts and are determined to keep "on the windy side of Care," [88] but neither will ever be a conventional literary lover, for in these two Shakespeare presents an attitude and a behavior pattern as real as that shown by Claudio and Hero.

In the well-known sonnet, "Loving in truth, and fain in verse my love to show," Sir Philip Sidney expresses seriously a critical view of conventional jargon which is similar to the nonserious objections of Benedick and Beatrice to the same thing. Fine inventions sought out in the works of other men are not the means whereby he may express his love for Stella. Benedick, attempting a poem in praise of Beatrice, is equally unable to employ the trite; but whereas Sidney concludes with, "Fool, said my muse to me, look in thy heart and write," [89] Benedick concludes with the acceptance of fact, "I cannot woo in festival terms." Sidney seeks a genuine expression of emotion and of course achieves it; Benedick is best described as a realist, or, as he says, "I do much wonder that one man, seeing how much another man is a fool when he dedicates his behaviors to love, will, after he hath laughed at such shallow follies in others, become the argument of his own scorn by falling in love. . . ." [90]

Both Sidney and Shakespeare reacted to the spate of love poetry utterly removed from reality, and such reaction was a perfectly normal development in the closing years of the century. A point of satiety, particularly in the imagery of amorous verse had been reached, so that new developments took the form of Donne's metaphysical style or Jonson's classicism. If we are to judge by Shakespeare's creation of Benedick and Beatrice, a new attitude came into being along with a new manner of expression. Exactly as Claudio and Hero are examples of the usual type of marriage as contrasted with the literary, so Benedick and Beatrice are another pair of realists sick to death of the jargon and extravagant behavior demanded by the fashionable code and so exhaustively exemplified, as we have seen, by such lovers as Beverley's Ariodant and Genevra. In Benedick and Beatrice, Shakespeare's tone is close to Raleigh's

> If all the world and love were young,
> And truth in every shepherd's tongue,
> These pretty pleasures might me move
> To live with thee and be thy love.[91]

Like the nymph who observes quite sagely that "flowers do fade" and

87. *Ibid.*, II, i, 343–344, 349–350.
88. *Ibid.*, II, i, 325–326.
89. Hebel and Hudson, *op. cit.*, p. 106.
90. *Much Ado*, II, iii, 7–12.
91. Hebel and Hudson, *op. cit.*, p. 137.

that "Time drives the flocks from field to fold," Beatrice is a realistic commentator:

. . . wooing, wedding, and repenting is as a Scotch jig, a measure, and a cinque-pace: the first suit is hot and hasty like a Scotch jig (and full as fantastical); the wedding mannerly modest (as a measure), full of state and ancientry; and then comes Repentance and with his bad legs falls into the cinque-pace faster and faster, till he sink into his grave.[92]

That Beatrice is not merely a shrew hating all men but is wise and observant is proved by Leonato's comment on the foregoing speech: "Cousin, you apprehend passing shrewdly," [93] or, as Beatrice says in reply, "I have a good eye, uncle; I can see a church by daylight." [94]

Benedick likewise "sees" quite clearly that love is not what it is in books. When Claudio says that Hero is the sweetest lady he ever looked on, Benedick replies, "I can see yet without spectacles and I see no such matter . . ." [95] Later, reflecting on the folly of love, he again uses the same figure: "May I be so converted and see with these eyes? I cannot tell; I think not. I will not be sworn but love may transform me to an oyster, but I'll take my oath on it, till he have made an oyster of me he shall never make me such a fool." [96] Like Beatrice, Benedick wishes to avoid the folly which they both see in the trite and conventional.

THE SIGNIFICANCE OF THE PLAY

In the opening section of this study it was suggested that an examination of the sources might offer a possible explanation of Shakespeare's purpose in combining the two plots, one borrowed and one original. In other words, it was my belief that the play had a unity of idea which had been obscured and which might be recovered if we could understand, in somewhat the way Shakespeare did, the implications of the source materials. It will be remembered that a definite growth and development was observed in the sequent retellings of the story. The lovers, their language, and their behavior grew sophisticated, and the narrative was deliberately complicated as various authors sought to portray the latest developments in that somewhat esoteric world of the literary amorists. Such characters in such a setting were the stock in trade of the poets and storytellers, but the interminable discussions of love which we find in such a play as *Endymion* or in such a novel as *Euphues,* the continuing refinement and elaborate extravagance of the conceits employed by the sonneteers could have but one conclusion—exhaustion by satiety. Whereas Sidney sought to

92. *Much Ado*, II, i, 76–83.
93. *Ibid.*, II, i, 84.
94. *Ibid.*, II, i, 85–86.
95. *Ibid.*, I, i, 191.
96. *Ibid.*, II, iii, 23–28.

break through the stifling convention to find and express a real and honest emotion, Shakespeare's reaction was one of amused ridicule. In the familiar sonnet, "My mistress' eyes are nothing like the sun," a series of revered and well-worn conceits are neatly reversed. Even such an antique and respectable conceit as the description of the beloved's hair as wires is here treated in cavalier fashion. Elsewhere Shakespeare, like Sidney, showed the gulf between convention and reality. Romeo in love with Rosaline is the conventional lover, but once he has fallen in love with Juliet he is a different person. The change is remarked by Mercutio who says, "Now art thou sociable, now art thou Romeo; now art thou what thou art by art as well as by Nature." [97] Whereas Romeo had previously exhibited all the proper symptoms, a love that is real produces quite a different effect.

In comedies the conventions are ridiculed as in the sonnets. Rosalind teases unmercifully an Orlando who has read all the right poets and knows just how a lover should behave. In *Twelfth Night* Orsino welters in the sorrowful enjoyment of his own emotions and everyone is in love with the wrong person. In *Love's Labour's Lost,* the princess of France and her ladies have a realistic suspicion of the sudden passions of Ferdinand and his lords, so they impose a penance which may well extinguish the frantic flames. "The lover, sighing like a furnace," had become absurd, and one could now laugh at the stale convention.

From such a point of view it was impossible for Shakespeare to regard seriously the prototypes of Hero and Claudio. Their story could, however, serve as the plot of a play, but the characters would have to be altered. As we have seen, the traditional lovers were transformed into a realistic young man seeking a good marriage and a dutiful daughter accepting without question the husband chosen by her father. As a matter of fact such characters are much better suited to the old story, particularly from a dramatic point of view, than are Timbreo and Fenicia. The main plot device, the stratagem of deception, poses something of a problem for a romantic lover. Believing his lady unfaithful, what is he to do? Revenge is unthinkable; in fact as we have seen in some versions, love is so powerful a force that the hero enters the lists against his own brother. But such a deception is the very thing to break a proposed mariage de convenance, for the considerations in such a match are economic and social. An unchaste bride is guilty of fraud and her falsity is well requited by a public denouncement of her. Such a scene is effective theater as Shakespeare demonstrates, and it is possible for Shakespeare to present it because he is dealing with a relationship quite alien to that involving romantic lovers. To the modern reader and to many critics the Temple scene is unpleasant and even brutal, but to Shakespeare's audience, fully cognizant of arranged marriages, there was no such reaction. In

97. *Romeo and Juliet,* II, iv, 92–94.

addition it should be remembered that any audience knows that every-thing will turn out satisfactorily.

One difficulty in using such a marriage situation for a comedy is the seriousness implicit in it. In a sense this plot could well result in a problem play like *All's Well,* and this aspect of the matter explains the critical disparagement of the main plot and of Claudio. If we will accept Eliza-bethan stereotypes we shall see that the situation is amenable to comic treatment, and it is here that Benedick and Beatrice become part of the idea of the play.

In the conclusion of the discussion of Benedick and Beatrice we noted the realistic attitude toward love which they both expressed. They are not really enemies of love; they are enemies of the dreary conventions. Whereas in the unreal world of romantic literature any woman would be overjoyed to accept the hand of such a prince as Pedro, Beatrice wisely rejects him. "No, my lord, unless I might have another for working days; your Grace is too costly to wear every day." [98] Her answer is not based on a hatred of men but on the realization that in the workaday world such a marriage would be impossible. Similar is her realistic de-scription of the Hero-Claudio marriage. "It is my cousin's duty to make curtsy and say, 'Father, as it please you'; but yet for all that, cousin, let him be a handsome fellow, or else make another curtsy and say, 'Father, as it please me.' " [99]

Benedick, likewise, is not so much a scorner of women ("my custom, as being a professed tyrant to their sex") as he is a scorner of false emo-tion. When Pedro prophesies that one day Benedick will "look pale with love," it is not love but the conventional pallor of the lover which Bene-dick denies. Just so in his soliloquy (II, iii, 6–38) it is foolish behavior of the romantic lover which rouses his ire. And finally, even though he so far yields to the convention as to attempt a poem to Beatrice, he cannot write one.

As Hero and Claudio represent one aspect of realism, so Benedick and Beatrice represent another. The former follow the way of the world where marriages are arranged by patrons or parents in contrast with the idyllic unions which literary convention followed exclusively. On the other hand Benedick and Beatrice are interested in an emotion which is real and a relationship based on reality instead of convention.

In other words Shakespeare's reinterpretation is basically a reaction to the ideas and characters of his sources. Instead of romantic lovers we have two couples completely opposed to the romantic tradition and these two couples are, in turn, representatives of opposite ideas: for the one, love is a real emotion, for the other, a business arrangement. But the play is not a *drame à thèse,* it is essentially high comedy wherein the frailty of

98. *Much Ado,* II, i, 340–342.
99. *Ibid.,* II, i, 55–59.

human pretensions is humorously revealed. Great plans are made by Claudio, Pedro, and Leonato; truculent attitudes are assumed by Benedick and Beatrice; but all comes to nought when the characters yield to temptation and eavesdrop. Through this recurrent device of overhearing Shakespeare secures a unity of tone, exactly as he had secured a unity of idea by emphasizing the essential realism of the characters in both plots. The final comic implication results from the fact that eavesdropping, the unintentional overhearing of Borachio by the Watch, is the means by which everything is set right. So it is with Benedick and Beatrice. Facing one another at the altar they finally yield when Claudio suddenly discovers Benedick's hidden sonnet, and Hero finds its counterpart written by Beatrice. Everything could have turned out quite differently but Shakespeare neatly manages the comic spirit and is amused, as we are, by the airy bubbles of pretensions, plans, and attitudes which are deflated with a laugh.

THE HISTORIE OF ARIODANTO AND IENEURA

BIBLIOGRAPHICAL NOTE

The sole extant copy of Peter Beverley's verse narrative is that printed without date by Thomas East for Fraunces Caldocke which is now in the possession of the Henry E. Huntington Library. This is a black letter octavo with the following collation: A-L⁸, M³. The title occupies A1ʳ with the verso blank. On A2ʳ begins a dedicatory letter to Peter Reade which concludes overleaf with mention of place and day: "From my chamber at Staple Inne, the first day of August." A3ʳ and A3ᵛ contain a prefatory letter, "To the Reader," while the text begins on A4ʳ. There is no pagination.

Our only external knowledge of the book is found in the following entry [1] in the Stationers' Register for the year from July 22, 1565, to July 22, 1566:

Recevyd of **henry Wekes** [Wykes] for his lycense for pryntinge of a/boke intituled *trage'gall and pleasaunte history*/ARIOUNDER . . ./JENEUOR the Daughter unto the kynge of . . . by PETER/BEVERLAY   iiijᵈ.

From this record it would seem that the poem had been written some time before July 22, 1566, but the exact date is uncertain. If the order of the entries is chronological, that is if the clerk recorded in sequence as MSS were brought in, then the Wykes entry would, by its position, seem to belong to the spring of 1566. If the dedicatory letter to Reade was a part of the original MS, then it could be dated as August 1, 1565, but since we do not know whether Wykes proceeded to print, during that summer, an edition which is now lost or whether the extant undated copy represents the first edition, there can be no conclusive dating of the letter. Indeed Beverley might have added the letter whenever the printing was finally planned.

What can be learned regarding the printers involved seems only to limit the date of publication within a few years. Thomas East purchased his freedom of the company on December 3, 1565,[2] and the first dated book bearing his name is Jehan Goeurat's *The Regiment of Life* translated by Thomas Phayre. This popular work had appeared in several editions and it is that of 1567 which East printed in conjunction with Henry Middleton.[3] In 1568 East printed three books which bear no name other than his [4] and one which he printed for Middleton.[5] Again in 1569 he printed for Middleton.[6] By 1570 East and Middleton were partners and they continued this relationship

---

1. *A Transcript of the Registers of the Company of Stationers,* ed. Edward Arber (5 vols., London, 1875–90), I, 312.

2. *Ibid.,* I, 317.

3. *Short Title Catalogue of Books Printed in England . . . 1475–1640* (London, Bibliographical Society, 1926), 11974. Hereafter referred to as *S.T.C.*

4. *S.T.C.,* 17250, 20956, 20957.

5. *S.T.C.,* 4028.

6. *S.T.C.,* 18949.

through 1571, 1572, and part of 1573.[7] In both 1572 and 1573 Middleton appears alone [8] and from 1573 until 1576 East operated independently,[9] but in 1576 the partnership was resumed.[10] The only other surviving book linking East with Caldocke is *Be Wise and Be Warned* which East printed for Caldocke in 1573.[11]

To judge by the foregoing evidence, East could have printed for Caldocke in 1565 or 1566 before he became associated with Middleton, or in 1568–69 when he was operating independently. It is unlikely that there would have been much more of a time interval than this between entry and printing. Actually when it is realized that Wykes printed for Caldocke in 1567 [12] and again in 1569,[13] it is possible to construct a hypothesis. The early years of the Register reveal little in the way of the transfer of rights and frequently books that were entered to one man were printed by another. Evidently such transfers were common and were a form of payment. Thus Caldocke might have secured the rights to *Ariodanto and Ieneura* from Wykes in return for the contract of printing books which Caldocke owned. Verse was not a particularly valuable commodity, and it may well be that the fledgling East was willing to undertake a work in which Wykes was not especially interested and which he had given or sold to Caldocke. From the available evidence, scanty though it is, it seems likely that East printed the poem in 1566.

An ultimate date of 1568 depends on the identity of "the Worshipfull M. Peter Reade" to whom Beverley addresses his dedicatory letter. It would seem that Reade was a man of some importance to judge from the tone of this letter with its "right Worshipful," "your worship," and its conclusion "Your Worshippe as his owne." A well-known Peter Reade is remembered by the following inscription on his monument in St. Peter's Mancroft, Norwich.

Here underlyethe y⁰ corps of Peter Rede Esquier who hath worthely served not only hys prynce and cuntry but allso the Emperor Charles the 5 bothe at the conquest of Barbaria and at the siege of Tunis as also in other places who had geven hym by the sayd Emperour for hys vallant dedes the order of Barbaria who dyed the 29 of December in the yeare of oure Lord God 1568.[14]

The Registers of St. Peter's contain the following burial entry for the year 1569:

Jann. 5   Mr Peter Reade Esquier of ye Citie of London [15]

7. *S.T.C.*, 2389, 4395, 11445, 11477, 23641, 24722, 4055, 4655.
8. *S.T.C.*, 700, 4846, 540, 10473, 12788, 13570, 25710.
9. *S.T.C.*, 7369, 19114, 21498, 11376, 11641, 19626, 21118, 25710.
10. *S.T.C.*, 6726.
11. *S.T.C.*, 21498.
12. *S.T.C.*, 23498.
13. *S.T.C.*, 13041.
14. I am indebted to Mr. L. G. Dodds, the verger of St. Peter's, who furnished me with a copy of the wording of the monument.
The date on the monument is given incorrectly as 1566 by Thomas Fuller (*The History of the Worthies of England*, ed. John Nichols [London, 1811], II, 133) and by John Weever (*Ancient Funeral Monuments of Great Britain* [London, 1631], p. 802).
15. Mr. Dodds has kindly supplied me with this information. The seemingly erroneous statement that Reade was buried in St. Sepulchre's Without Cripplegate, London,

Reade came from a prominent Norwich family, his father, Edward, having been four times mayor of the city. He married twice, first, Jane, the daughter of Sir Anthony Lea, and after her death, Ann, the daughter of Sir Thomas Blenerhassett.[16] His benefactions included the gift of a fine salt to the city [17] and a bequest of certain houses, the income from which was to insure "that the great bell in St. Peter's Mancroft Church should be rung at four o'clock in the morning and eight in the evening forever; for the help and benefit of travellers." [18]

That this Peter Reade was Peter Beverley's patron is proved by the terms of Reade's will. A codicil to this will made on December 18, 1568, bequeaths an annuity of £6 a year to be paid to "Peter Beverlaye, my godsonne." [19] The relationship is tantalizing : there obviously must have been some connection between the families, but so far as I have searched, no other evidence is available. But it is clear that the dedicatory letter must have been written on or before August 1, 1568, because after that date Beverley would have spoken of his deceased godfather. Even though a terminal date is thus established, I incline to the date of 1566 for East's printing of the poem.

derives from Harley MS 1177, fol. 175ᵛ. This MS is a transcript of the 1561 Visitation of Suffolk made in 1618 by Samuel Lennard, Bluemantle Poursuivant. Obviously the original visitation could not have contained a notice of Reade's burial, so we can only conclude that Lennard was misinformed.

16. Harl. MS 1177, fol. 175ᵛ.
17. H. J. Dukinfield Astley, *Memorials of Old Norfolk* (London, 1908), p. 65.
18. *Norfolk Lists from the Reformation to the Present Time* (Norwich, 1837), p. 168.
19. Perogative Court of Canterbury, 4 Sheffeld.

BIOGRAPHICAL NOTE

The only information which Peter Beverley has vouchsafed us is the fact that he resided in Staple Inn, and the only other literary work which we may ascribe to him is the commendatory poem which he wrote for Geoffrey Fenton's *Tragical Discourses*.[1] A Peter Beverley matriculated as a pensioner at St. John's College, Cambridge, in the Michaelmas term of 1553. He had transferred to Clare College by 1556–57 when he took his B.A. and he was subsequently a fellow of Clare.[2] Whether this Cambridge don was the author of *The Historie of Ariodanto and Ieneura* is by no means certain, but he is the only Peter Beverley whom I have been able to find who might reasonably be assumed to have literary interests. The fact that this poem marks the first English appearance of any portion of the *Orlando Furioso* is highly significant in this connection. Beverley either read the original Italian or made use of one of the French translations. He thus had some linguistic ability and an interest in foreign literature, although he never indicates that he has borrowed his materials from Ariosto. The verses in Fenton's *Tragical Discourses* also show that Beverley was in a literary circle, for the other contributors include George Turbervile whose *Epitaphes, Epigrams, Songs, and Sonets* was printed in 1567 and Sir John Conway, the author of *Meditations and Praiers* (1570). Conceivably Beverley might be the "P.B." who contributed commendatory verses to Gascoigne's *Posies* (1575). He could have known Gascoigne at Cambridge or later in London through their mutual association with the Inns of Court. Clearly our poet cannot be the Peter Beverley, yeoman, of Wheldrake, Yorkshire, who died in 1582 and whose will is extant in the York Registry.[3] He may, however, be the Peter Beverley who in 1584 was coplaintiff with William Beverley in a Yorkshire Feet of Fines action concerning property in East Haslerton and Hollow Carr.[4] Both plaintiffs are described as "gent.," and as I shall show there is reason to believe that the poet came from Yorkshire. There are Beverleys in other counties, but, as far as I have searched, the only ones bearing the Christian name "Peter" are those noted above.

One possible clue may be found in the association with St. John's College. Five other Beverleys were also at John's between 1583 and 1598. Two of these were Vincent and John, sons of Thomas Beverley of Selby, Yorkshire, and they matriculated *ca.* 1594. The counties of origin for the other

1. *Certain Tragical Discourses of Bandello Translated by Geffraie Fenton Anno 1567*, ed. Robert Langton Douglas (2 vols., London, 1898), I, 15–16.
2. J. and J. A. Venn, *Alumni Cantabrigenses* (Cambridge, 1922), I, 146.
3. *Index of Wills in the York Registry 1568–85, Yorkshire Archaeological Society, Record Series*, XIX (1895), 15.
4. *Feet of Fines of the Tudor Period*, Pt. III, *York. Arch. and Top. Asso., Record Series*, VII, 20.

Johnians are unknown, but it may well be that they also came from Yorkshire and that there was a connection between the family and the college. The possibility that the Peter Beverley of St. John's was a Yorkshire man may be related to the fact that in *The Historie of Ariodanto and Ieneura* there survive evidences of a northern dialect. The noun "beck," meaning a brook, is a northern form and such rhymes as "Diamond-found," "friend-minde," and "region-wonne-towne" indicate a definite northern pronunciation. The use of "til" meaning "while," and "wear" meaning "spend," and the form "judges" for the imperative "judge" is further evidence of a northern dialect. A consistent spelling of several words enforces the foregoing: "geve" is regularly used for "give," "skrykes" or "skreekes" for "shrieks," "searke" for "search," "entrald" for "enthralled," "vanquist" for "vanquisht," "tomled" for "tumbled," and "thought" for "though." [5] While none of this is in the least conclusive, it may be suggested that our author was a Yorkshireman, that he was a student of St. John's College, Cambridge, and that remnants of his origin survive in the printed text of the poem.

Whatever his identity and however bad his poem, Beverley is worthy of some consideration. He knew and adapted the *Orlando* and was the first Englishman to make use of this epic. Furthermore, he knew very well the narrative standards and ideals of his own age, since we find in him those same instincts which animated the work of Painter and Fenton. In a sense he looked forward as we may perceive by reflecting on his thorough-going exploitation of the love conventions and language which were to be so much a part of the literature which followed.

5. My colleagues, Professors Helge Kökeritz and E. T. Donaldson, have been good enough to examine the evidence and give me the benefit of their philological knowledge of the period.

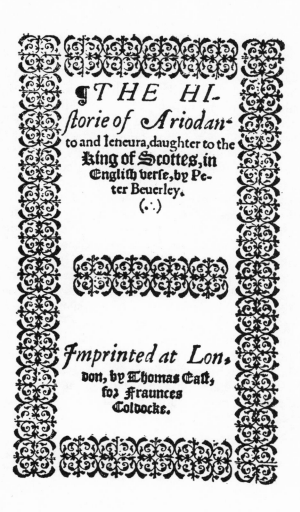

¶THE HI-
storie of Ariodan-
to and Ieneura, daughter to the
King of Scottes, in
English verse, by Pe-
ter Beuerley.
(∴)

Imprinted at Lon-
don, by Thomas East,
for Fraunces
Coldocke.

To the Worshipfull M. Peter

Reade, Peter Beverley, wisheth
perfect felicitie.

IF I had thought (right Worshipful) that Slaunders tongue could greter
have envied this my rude Booke, then the show of my good will heereby
unto you, shoulde ease my desirous mynde, I would then have stayed this
bould enterprise, which with hasarde of good report I have attempted.
But such is the affection of a well meaning harte, that sooner it offers
it self to the spightfull blotte of scornefull defame, then desire should
want eyther by signe or deede, to requite received benefittes. The tossed
barke, seld findes the desired porte, without the stormes of the aire, the
surges of the sea, and the force of the enemie : and it is as harde for the
idell marchant to encrease his stocke, as it is for the cowarde Knight to
gaine lastinge memorie : So harde it is for me (whose abilitie is as well
[A2ʳ] knowen to your worship, as to my selfe) without the / poysoned
hate of the stinking tongue, the malicious scornes of the envious head, and
the dispightfull scoffes of the shamelesse countenance, to advertise you
of my desirous mind, ready at all times to pleasure you. The enfection of
whose filthie jawes, I have rather chosen by happie adventure to escape,
then by lurking silence, still to remaine an unknowen welwiller. This onely
resteth, and this is it which seekes to staye my hastie hande : The simple-
nes of the gifte, whiche if you regard not, but thinke well of the willing
giver, I live happie, nought fearing the force of scornes blast. Thus wish-
inge to your worshippe happie health, wealth to the best contentation of
your harte, lasting life, and to me (yours) abilitie once to answer your
great curtesie. I end. From my chamber at Staple Inne, the first day of
August.

Your Worshippe as his
[A2ᵛ]   owne Pe. Beverley.

To the Reader.

TO thy frendly acceptance, (gentle Reader) more boldly than advisedly,
I have offred here yᵉ unripe fruits of my barren orchard, the bitter taste
wherof, is more liker to annoy thy sugred lippes, then please thy longing
minde. But see as by diligent searche, the labouring Bee fyndes the wholsome honie amydst the infective hearbe : So maiest thou (if thou list
indifferently to reade, and carefullye to marke) happe the sage advise of

good counsell, and learne by others mischiefs to shunne thine owne
decay. Thou knowest within the harde shell shrowdeth the sweet curnell,
and amongst pricking thornes the fragrant Rose is fostred, within the
hard flint (they say) the precious Diamound is found, & amongst the
unperfectnes of my rude vers, the force of treason is showed and his juste
desert. If thou canst by falshood learne / to shunne disceite, I have [A3ʳ]
my wish, and thou happy. If juste revenge for foule offence can admonish
thee to serve God, obey thy Prince, no doubt, but thou shalt live an honest
life, and die thrise blessed.

Through twoo fieldes thy waye is directed, the one full of briars, hath
the perfect path to felicitie: the other (more pleasant to the vicious
minde) leades to endles miserie: choose with advise, and shunne with
discretion. And to me thy unknowen friend, lende (I praye thee) as
friendly judgement, as I shall wyshe for thy prosperous estate.

Farewell.

[A3ᵛ]

Ariodanto, and Jenevra

AMongst the vanquisht Regions, that worthy brute did winne:
There is a soyle in these our dayes, with Occean Seas cloasde in.
That fertile is, and peopled well, and stord with pleasant fieldes:
And hath for tillage lucky land, that yeerly profit yeeldes.
Within ye land sometime ther dwelt a King of noble fame:
Whose actes wer such, as gaind to him an everlasting name.
Who, when he Cepter long had held and ruled his realme with right:
In quiet rest, in spight of foe, and force of friendles might.
Did take to wife a noble Dame, of egall Parentage:
Of bewty great, of vertues more, and of a youthfull age.
By whom he had a Daughter fayre, that joyed his aged yeares:
And plesure great at length did bring unto his hoary heares.
This child as time gan passe from her, so bewty doth increase:
And as in yeeres she gan to grow so vertues to her prease.
Of shape and seemly favour, she lackt nought that nature could
In goodliest wise bestow of her, or frame in fayrest mould.   [A4^r]
To this such giftes of heavenly hew, full fraught with courtly grace:
And modest mirth, eke gentle mynd presaging royall race.
That who excels Jenevora, (for so this Lady hight:)
Or who more bewtifull then she, or pleasde more eche sight.
For proufe behould how swift report doth brute in forren land:
This Princes name, her shape & hew of eche estate is scand.
The Kings that joyne unto her syre, do seeke her grace to winne:
The Ladies eke that vertues love, to serve her grace beginne.
But see farre of in Italie this Ladies name is blown:
And ther her gifts of naturs art, to all are lively known.
Where at that time two gentlemen of honest family:
Italians both by birth and bloud and brothers there did lie.
The eldest namd Lurcanio, that speare and sheld desird:
The other eke Ariodant, that more to love aspierd.
These two y^t long had lived at home, and lothd with Idle life:
And moved eke with this report, that every where is rife.   [A4^v]
Are now agreed to leave this ease, theyr frendes and native soyle:
And minde to seke adventures farre with wery travels toyle.
And therfore first their land they sel, for present paiment tould:
And other goods they do convert, (for cariage light) to gould.
This don, their busines eke dispatcht and hevy parting past:
From wailing friends that wo their wil, they leave the towne at last.
And passe ye mountains hie unknown and seke the desert dales:
And scape by guyde the raggy rocks and tread the trodden vales.
Thus when theyr werie steps had scapte, a thousand daungers past:

And that they needes must leave the land, and yeld to sayle and mast.
To Neptunes wil they doo commit them selves, and then do pray:
The maister for to guide his shippe, to Scottish Realme the way.
So said, he keepes his bidden course, and hath a gale at will:
The mariner at ease also, his part doth well fulfill.
So long these werie travelers, are tost with sea and winde:
That now the long desired port, and wyshed soyle they finde.   [A5ʳ]
Then nought there is but hale and pull, the Ancars are out cast:
The maister hath his earned hyre, and prayes their life longe last.
This don, the brothers aske the way that leadeth to the Court:
Wheras the noble king of Scottes, doth keepe his Royall port.
Which known, with speede they seeke to see, and in theyr travell, they
Devise their tale, theyr whole request and chieflye, how they may
Get intertainment in the Court, and how Lurcanio:
Should spokeman be for both, but see whilst talking thus they go,
The wavering vanes of gleming golde, that Phebus caused to shine:
Appere, and reard up walles on hie, that fed theyr gredy eyen.
They see the carved turrets tops, they see the regall place:
The sight wherof had forst them run a wery wandring race.
Thus are these straungers happely, arrived at the Court,
Wheras this peerles Dame abides, of whome ringes this report.
There walke they forth with comly grace and enter in the hall,
Where after greating, they declare, what chaunce had them befall. [A5ᵛ]
To seeke that lande: their names they tel, and eke of whence they are:
This tould, one shewes unto the king of two arived theare.
And woord for woord, as he had hard he tells, and eke there state
And comlines he hideth not: Besides he doth dilate.
Their friendly gretings, and their talke: this sayde, he kneling staies.
The king that pawsing with him selfe, and waying divers wayes,
What harme mought lightly him ensue, if such he should retaine,
As under cloke of frendship, mought put him and his to payne:
I meane as mought spye out the strength of all his region:
And eke what corner weakest weare, and easiest to be wonne.
And so when he in age should thinke, to leade a surest lyfe:
They should him force through their deceit, to ende his daies in strife.
These thoughts, this wise and warie prince, doth ponder in his braine
Long tyme, and in these doughtfull fitts, he silent doth remaine.
Yet mindes he not to let them part, till what they would were knowen:
And till the cause of their arive, were plainely to him showen.   [A6ʳ]
Wherfore he doth bid call to him, these straungers twoo in haste:
That banisht have their native soile, in his court to be plast.
Which message done, these brothers two, as men nothing dismaied:
To speake before the Emperour, whom earst they had obeied.
Present themselves before the king, wher after silence done:

Lurcanio in their two names, thus hath his tale begonne.
THat king, that first gave life to you, increase your happie daies:
(Oh king) and keepe your noble court, from force of foes alwayes.
Whilest we Italian brothers two, in Italy dyd dwell:
And whilste with ease we past the time, as chaunce and times befel.
Behould report that wandring flies, in every region:
Resound your name and worthines, at last unto the towne
Wher we abode consuming time in drousie idelnes:
And spending aye our youthful yeres in irksum quietnes.
These childish toies thus lothd (I say) these newes agreing eke
With us, that thought ech day a month till we the bands mought
   breke.   [A6ᵛ]
Of this long discontented lyfe, we doo forthwith agree
All needfull things at home dispatcht, this court of yours to see
And there if we mought favor get, and grace likewise obtaine:
To serve your highnes faithfully, and loyall to remaine:
Til death we minde. This forst hath us (O king) to leave our port:
Our frends, our goods, our kinsmen al to whom we were comfort.
In hope to be retaind of you, which is our whole request:
Wherin we trust for to performe, that seemes a courtier best.
The king that wel had markt his tale his countnaunce and his grace:
And saw him feawtred well of lims and of a warlike face.
And praysing long within him selfe, the yongest brothers chere:
That sober was presaging truth, forthwith doth banish feare.
And biddes these wery travelers, welcome unto the place
Desired long. And intertaines, them both with friendly grace.
Into his court, commaunding them, all falshood to expell:
And geves them pencions yerely, wherwith they may live well.   [A7ʳ]
Thus are these glad Italians, new courtiers both become:
That seeke eche way to purchase love as well of all as some.
THe king that for disport doth use, oft times for to pursue:
The dreadfull [chase] of grislie beastes, so Idle lyfe t'eschue:
Commaunds the hunt prepared be, the morow next by prime:
And that eche one appareld be, in armes against that tyme,
To waite upon his highnes then that will on hunting go:
And eke with him the strangers two he doth commaund also.
The night is past, and Sopor flies, and in his steede Aurore
Doth show hir gladsome countenance and for to joy the more
Eche sight, sir Phebus golden raies, from east beginnes tappeare,
Then nought ther is within the court, but trudging here and there.
Sum saddels fit, sum armour scoure sum bridell foming steede:
And sum do wheat the steeled glaive to give the Beare his meede.
Sum trapers trim, sum couple dogs sum weare in steede of steele,
A maled coate, with armed sword, to make his enmies reele.   [A7ᵛ]

The pages trimme theyr lords in haste, the hunt cries lowde away :
The steedes are foorth, that stamping fast, on champing bit do play.
The werbling note the hunter blowes, the king on courser strydes :
The lusty rought of knights make hast, that priking forward glydes.
The hunt is up, the game is founde, eche seekes a divers waye :
The noble rought of Chevalrie, dispersed now doo stray.
Some here do meete the tusked bore some findes the Lyberd stout :
Some do encounter with the Beare some rouse of Harts a route.
Thus dog and man is occupied, him selfe for to defend :
And for to gaine a lasting name, doo sturdie strokes foorth send.
The king in [chase] hath lost his mates, and in his wandring, hee
Findes, out a lothsome Lion coucht that monstrous was to see.
Wherto he makes a thundring course with speare well set in rest :
The Lyon rampant meetes the staffe, that it to shevers brest.
Then glaive he drawes like noble knight, and strikes with courage stout :
And prickes, and breathes, and strikes again, as one devoide of
    doubte,   [A8ʳ]
But all in vayne those strokes are spent his traunchser, nought doth
    carve,
But either slydes from side to side, or in his hand doth Swarve.
Wher at, he halfe agast doth feare, least he were put to shame :
And least his former worthines, should ende with vanquisht name.
Wherfore he mightely defends him selfe from Lions clawes,
That raseth all attayned to with those his persing pawes.
Yet warely warding sith he could nothing prevaile in strength,
But ward, & stroke, are bootles spent when down he must at length.
Thus as the Lion had the best, and almost won the feelde :
Adventure drove Lurcanio with Speare in hand and sheelde
To seeke that place, but when he saw his soveraigne at the wurst,
No boote to byd him spurre his steede and to the battell thrust.
For first he knightly brake his speare and after drawes his blade,
Wherwith within a moments space, a large wound he had made,
Upon the Lions shoulder bone, that caused him for to kneele :
And then his head he carved of and so made him to reele :   [A8ᵛ]
The king delivered thus from death, by stout Lurcanio,
With thousand thankes imbrased him in both his armes also.
Tyll that his menne had found him out, to whom he hideth nought :
But how he nigh confounded was, and how the straunger fought.
In his defence so valiantlie, and with so mightie force,
That after many mortall woundes, he parted head from corse.
Now is report new occupied, in blasing martiall feates :
Wherwith the court so pressed is, that up to Skies it beates.
And flies to towne both farre and neare : and nowe ascendes againe,
And putteth fame to werie toyle, and to an endles payne.

But to returne, the king is horst, that doth for werines :
Leave of the chase, then homeward all theyr divers happes expresse.
Thus talking, are these hunters come unto the Pallas gates,
Where eche disarmes his werie bones, and welcomes home his mates.
There nought is talkt within the Court, but of the straungers might
And how he noblie savde their liege, and kild his foe in fight.   [B1ʳ]
The Ladies doo extoll this act, up to the cloudie skies :
The knightes by heapes of his great strokes doo diversly devise.
The night renewes his carefull course, Titan is lodgd in west,
All seekes their soft and quiet bed their wery bones to rest.
Ariodant (that longs to see this long desired Dame)
Is also coucht in tumbling bed, where he records her name.
A thousand times, & thus consumes halfe Junos wanny race :
And if he slepe, he dreams strait ways of that most heavenly face.
The Cock crowes forth his dawning note : the day starres shewes in east,
The Nightingale the gladsom tunes sings out with cheerfull brest.
The courtiers rise that use disportes, as pleaseth best their will,
Some Hauks reclayme, some Coursers ride and some do daunce their fill.
Some joye in reading Histories, and some in Musikes art,
Thus time is spent in comly sports, as pleaseth best their hart.
Now is the King at dinner set, there waytes Ariodant,
That is the seemliest of them all, and one that nought doth want. [B1ᵛ]
Of natures craft, by whom the King doth send a coverd mease :
To Princes faire Jenevora, that is his lifes increase.
This message doth Ariodant, performe in seemliest wies :
Who kneeling doth the cates present before her cristall eyes.
The Lady thanks the messenger, and gives him in reward :
A costly gem, which he receives, but nought he doth regard.
The gift so much, as that her looke, which is so fixt in hart :
That from that time he holds it fast, till lyfe from lims doo part.
And she againe (that marked hath so well his comly face :
His shape, his vew, his countnance grave, and eke his semely grace.)
Sayes in her hart this same is he whom I in brest will shrine :
Till sisters three with fatall reele my vitall webbe untwine.
Thus Venus child hath tainted two with his sharpe persing dart :
And yet unknowen to both it is, how eche joyes others hart.
Ariodant that clokes (I say) this hote new kindled fire :
(His dutie done) departs agayne, with gayne of double hire.   [B2ʳ]
And makes his wayting very short, and shunnes the tast of meate,
And to his chamber hies in hast, to coole his scorching heate :
Ther doth he oft record her talke, he sees her smiling cheare,
He sees those colours angellyke, he sees her glistring heare.
He viewes (he thinkes) those Rubie [lippes] that thankt him for his
    payne,

He feeles (he thinkes) those azurd vaynes that gave him that great
    gayne:
But when he sees he is deceivd, a thousand sighes departe,
With flouds of teares, and deadly sobbes out from his carefull hart.
And thus begins a long discours of this new tasted fit,
Which as I can I shall declare, thou Pallas guide my wit.
From whence proceedes this pinching payne, and griefes of deadly smart?
Or els what act hath chaunged thus (oh foole) thy joyfull hart,
That thus thou lothst those pleasant sports, that here in Court are usd,
And seekst a drousie caban couch thy wonted myrth refuse?
Tell what hath made this soden chaunge, bewray these griefes of minde,
The pacient, when the wound is greene, a salve doth soonest finde. [B2ᵛ]
A salve Alas. it is booteles wynd, Its death that must me cure:
My wound doth festred lye in hart, and will till life endure.
(Oh foole) that so wert fed with fame, such toyle to undertake
For her, that nought doth rue thy care, ne sorowes none will make.
For thee, and yet shee is the cause, that thus thou doest susteine,
These griping griefes of grisly death which will for aye remayne.
Oh cruell happe and destenie, oh wight unfortunate,
Oh cative vile, unhappe thrise, and borne to cruell fate.
What joy did take thy idell brayne, when thou didst see her face,
Thus to be trapt with heapes of griefe in so short time and space.
Oh Cokadrill of Venus shape why hast thou thus beguild?
The wyght, that for thy fame him selfe from nature soile exyld.
But how is that knowen unto her whom blameles I accuse?
Or why should I uncivill beast that worthie shape abuse?
Whose outward shewe presageth truth, and store of courtesie,
As lately by her great reward was showd sufficiently.   [B3ʳ]
No, no, it is he that workes my woe, who forceth Kinges to love,
That blindly shotes his poysned dart from stately throne above.
That Cupide stroke mi senceles ghost full well I know, when I
Beheld that goodly countenaunce, with two fast persing eye.
Wherfore his dome I must obey, though love [unegall] be:
And though I spend my youthfull dayes in this vile misery.
This dolefull tale, thus tould, the teares proceede from swelling eyes:
By streames, and now the greevous grons increase his wofull cries.
Now hope revives his dying limmes, dispayre now drives in death:
And now doth feare make sences faile, and stoppe his vitall breath.
Thus long he spends a lingring lyfe, and craves a happy day:
Or els he wils by greedy grave, his last fate for to pray.
But to speake of Jenevora, and to recount her fittes:
And how in closet she doth fare, as one bereved of wittes:
My pen shuld rather moisture want to write that I intend:
Then store of cares for to dilate, that would whole volumes spend. [B3ᵛ]

For after she had knowen his name, and how an aliant borne
He was, her hart began to coole, as one welny forlorne.
And thus with faultring tounge shee sayd, why sekest thou lenger life:
That by this act deservest death, with point of bloudy knife.
Oh cative vyle, and vylest wretch, that liveth under skyes:
And may not race of Royall bloud, thy foolish mynd suffice?
Nor noble lyne of Scottish soyle wher thou mayst chuse a feare:
Thy childish will at full content, but thou must hold him deare.
That hath throgh theft exild him selfe or els by murdring hand:
Estrangd him from his carlish kin, and now seeks forren lande?
Wilt thou assotted be of him, that like a wandring slave:
Is come unto thy fathers court, some livelihood to have?
What, seekst thou to shame thy selfe, and to abuse thy kinne?
And myndst thou thus to purchase hate, in hope a slave to winne.
A slave. Oh spitefull sting of hate, for Ladies farre unfitte:
Why doo I thus with poysned words, misuse my praysid wit.   [B4ʳ]
Why should I terme him felon eke that is so gratious:
Or els of murder him accuse that is so curteous?
Why do I live to call him slave that is the comliest wight,
That ever scapte from natures handes or ever past my sight?
And if that lackt, his brothers deede would show his race right well,
Whose worthie rescue of the King doth make his name excell.
Therfore as I am Princesse true, I vow Ariodant.
By him that Skies and Earth did frame and trees and herbes did plant,
Til life doth leave my careful corpse to love thee faithfullie,
As ever Lady loved her feere, in spite of vyle adversitie.
She sayd, and down to ground she falles in sound, and drawes no breath
Long time, as one that had resind her life to wished death.
And when she doth revive againe, the stilling teares depart
Like silver droppes from drowned eyes, and gastlie sighes from hart.
Thus leaves she Ladies companie, and shunnes eche kind of sport,
In steed wherof, to desert walkes, shee dayly doth resort.   [B4ᵛ]
Where sundrie thoughts opresse her mind: now feare for to obtayne
Like love of him, for whom she doth, these passions hard susteine:
And now the Kings consent she feares, whose hest she must obey,
And eke whose mynd is chiefly bent tencrease her state eche way.
These arguments full fraught with doubt are rife within hir brayne,
And if she finde one pleasant thought a thousand griefes remayne.
Like fittes doo faint Ariodant, that wandring here and there:
Can finde no place to ease his paine, nor damp his doughts of feare.
Wherfore his bloud consumes away, his fleshe to boanes doo fade,
His colour whan as clod of clay most like a senselesse shade.
The youthfull sutes which earst he ware unworne doo lye in chest,
And now the black and tawny hew doth please this heavy gest.

In fine, these fittes so much annoye his wery irksum life:
That now he seekes unhappie man, to fall on persing knife.
Lurcanio, that marks this change, and sees with woo this state:
And feares least that he mought bewayle his brothers griefe to late. [B5ʳ]
Spies out at length both tyme, and place, for to discharge his mynde
To him, and listing [eare] required, spends thus his boteles winde.
HOw long shall these consuming fittes increase thy brothers griefe:
From whom (unkind) thou hidst thy cares, that seekes for thy reliefe.
What meanes (I say) these pyning paines, whence springs these fluddes
    of care:
What fever fit hath forced thee, thus ruthfully to fare?
Why speakest thou not? why stayes thy toung disclose thy long disease.
And wylt thou thus with shortning dayes the heavenly ghostes displease?
If sicknes do opresse thy corps, then physicks counsel use,
If fond conceytes of matters past, do forse thee for to muse,
And shun the joyes that here be used, then seeke swete musikes art,
Which wil (they say) all heavy dumps, to joyfull fittes convart.
Perhaps the ayre of this land, thy nature doth dytest:
And makes thee thus to feele disease, and taste unquiet rest.
If that it be, no feare of death, tyme wyll weare that away,
As earst it did, when in the Seas this part we learnd to play.   [B5ᵛ]
But what doth meane this mourning weede and lothsome tawnie hew,
As though thou hadst thy fredom lost, to serve fond Venus crewe.
If so thou hast, advise thee well, so choyse be egall plaste,
Beware in tyme, shunne froward dame, least wind, and woords be wast.
By proufe I say (my brother) I, this lesson short is trewe.
The Faulkner seld is suer of Hauke, till she be close in mewe.
Therfore let wittes be guid to deedes, thou warnd mayst learn to lyve,
Shun thraldoms yocke thy brother biddes, that doth this councell give.
Ariodant that hard this speache, but reason nought esteemed,
With strayned voice thus answer made, as one with care consumd,
(As you have sayd my brother deare) a lothsome lyfe I leade,
But whence, or wher, or how it comes tis hid from me in deede.
No quartaine fit hath freated me, ne fury fond of mynd,
Ne change of skyes, but gods above, this plage have just assignd,
For my fore passed dayes in sinne, wherfore let this content,
Thy doutfull head, sith just it is which Jove himselfe hath sent.   [B6ʳ]
Think you these toyes of veneire should lodge within my braine:
Or Ladies love in hope to win, should make me thus sustaine
Those scorching griefes, and pyning paines, and stormes of deadly smart?
No, no, those fittes most ferdest be from my unskilfull heart.
Wherfore, in hope, I thus conclude, as sinne did smart deserve,
So Jove that high and mightie God, from pitie will not swerve.
This answer made, Lurcanio departs with pleased mind,

Now doughting least but word for word as he had hard to find.
Ariodant (that nought was moved to leave his wanted woes.
For brothers words to whom his love he hates for to disclose)
Doth still consume a wery lyfe, with endles griping payne,
And dayly feare augments his doole least love be voud in vayne.
Besides thinks he, if she should yelde like love to my desert:
And then by love unegall we should foresed be to part:
These eyes should never see againe the rayes of Titans lyght,
But poyson strong, or bathed blade, my desprat death should dight. [B6ᵛ]
But yet if she would rue my care, I forst not Princely might:
For rather then the love should slacke, we sure would make a flight.
And better it is in my conceit, to live in povertie
With joye, then in these cancred cares, to tast flouddes of prosperitie.
For joye bryngs health to aged limmes, when cares consume the corse,
And joy doth make leng lyfe to men, when couples care devorse.
What profits welth to lyve in woe, what gaynes possessions great,
When heart is vext continually with cares of firie heat?
The best and happie state I count in this unstable lyfe:
Is pleasure plast with quietnes, devoyde of stormes of stryfe.
Should we then let in hope to finde this wished jolitie:
To leave a Princies Pallas fraught with this vyle miserie.
And ist not better toyle for pence with willyng sweat of browe,
And laboryng hand to dyg and delve, or els to dryve the plowe:
And then when labour finisht is to sit by tosting fyre:
And sing, and whystle mirely, with gaine of earned hyre?   [B7ʳ]
Then here in court to goe as brave, as rayes of glistrying Sunne:
And have a hart that dayly seekes, his vital breath to shunne?
Besides what shame can turn to us, to live in soyle not known:
For banisht wights, but laboring soules, to toyle to keepe our owne.
Oh that these woords mought once procede from those thy rubie lippes:
Whose countnuance, shape, and comlines, hath forst me feele these fittes.
For at the least till thou shalt take some pitie of my care:
These griefs, & pangs of wished death my ghost will never spare.
Thus makes his faltring tongue an end, and he on tumblyng bed
Doth cast his weake and wery lyms, wher now from troubled head
Doth passe, & soft & slumbring sleape, and now in dreame appeare,
Two ladies dect with robes of gould that purpure [vanes] do weare:
Upon their heads two crowns they had, well set with precious stone,
And in their hand Jenevora, that semd to make great mone.
Thus past they foorth with stately steps, and now approch the place
Where he doth lye, and thus begins the one with seemly grace.   [B7ᵛ]
BEhould thine owne, (Ariodant,) whome cares of love do kill,
Whose lyfe and death thou skillesse houldst, to save or els to spill.
At length let pitie placed be, within thy friendly brest,

That she may gaine, & thou not lose, the fruits of wished rest.
(Quod she), and than the other sayd, How long shall freating payne
Consume her Rosiat colour that all earthly shapes doth staine.
See here unkynd, whilst thou dost sleape, and take thy quiet ease,
Jenevora doth feele for thee the fittes of vile disease.
Wherfore dispatch, cast sleape away bryng health to her againe:
That since she first dyd see thy corps, hath felt this pyning paine.
These words had scarsly left hir lips when they wear out of sight:
And he that care had choked nie, and fedde with great delight,
To see his Ladie and his love, in presence face to face,
And gone againe so sodainly, before he could imbrace
Her tender limmes, these sights I say hath forst him to awake:
But when he knowes it is a dreame an out crie he doth make,   [B8ʳ]
As though his hart had felt the stroke, of fiers untimely death,
And lyke as it to loftie Skies, he hath resingde his breath.
And doth it not suffise (quoth he) a wakyng wight to wrong,
With heapes of undeserved paynes, and fittes of death among.
But dreames, and fond alusions two, must help for to augment,
My scorching cares that long or this, my life had welnye spent?
Oh frowning [gods] and merciles, that seeke to feede my vayne,
With fond perswasions, that my love is quite with love againe,
These eyes saw my Jenevora, that seemd to pyne away.
Because she ferd to joy my love, as Ladies two dyd say
Which were the heavenliest creatures that erst myne eyes dyd see,
Bedect with gold, & crowns they had and suer Gods they bee.
Oh blessed sight, and joyful newes, to good for troth I feare:
And may it be that thou thus farest for him that houlds the deare.
Then fye of care, and farewel couch, rejoyce in joye my hart,
For then within my skyn shal lodge no more this dayly smart.   [B8ᵛ]
But why should I thus trust in dreames that fansies be of mynde:
And eke unconstant groundes of troth, as writers have definde.
At least a dreame is contrary, and then to true in deede
It is, that lothsome loves dispayre my griping griefes doth feede.
Yet Poets say that dreames be true and things to come foreshowes,
For profe, they tel a doleful dreame, that Creasides ghost well knows.
And wast not tould Andromaka, in vision plaine by night:
That Hector shuld the morow next, depart from life by sight?
If Poetes fayle, let Scripture serve, and did not Pharao dreame:
What gret increase, & derth likewise should happe unto this Realme?
And Joseph saw in slumbring sleape, what honour should befall
To him, and how his brothers shefes, before his shefe did fall.
These prove yᵉ dreame is messenger of good and bad ensue:
As warning sent from God above these sinfull deedes teschue.
Therfore in hope of happie hap, dispayre I do defie:

And henceforth bouldly I do intend to seeke some remedie.   [Cɪʳ]
And if such lotte belotted me, as I may her injoye,
No more these cares I do protest, my sences shall annoy.
Now is the pacient plaister layd, to his long fretted wound :
And now his wits he cals to him, to helpe with counsell sound.
He leaves those careful couches now he seekes to salve his sore,
As one that shunnes the furious meates, instruct by Phisickes lore.
The desert walkes which earst he trod, are desert now for him :
And now remembraunce of his dreame rejoyseth in every limme.
In fine his care doth now consist, only for to disclose :
His fittes unto Jenevora, and his long tasted woes.
Wherin so wisely he hath wrought, and playd so well his part :
That now by life or els by death, to ease his loden hart.

                         a meanes he findes.

WHen Cupid had with poysned dart, performed his full intent,
Upon these sillie lovers twoo, and forst them to consent.
(Unknown to both,) unto his lore, by mutuall burning love :
He left eche wayling others chaunce, and clymes to skies above.   [Cɪᵛ]
But she alas (whose colour shewes, the passions of her mynde :)
Stayes not to wayle her bitter chaunce, with teares and wasted winde.
And still complaynes in secret wise, of this consuming fit :
Which for to ease, she cries to death, her hart in hast to flit.
The Ladies crave by gentle meanes to know her cause of care :
But she (with skill) nought more than that detesteth to declare.
The night is past with tumbling oft within her wery bed :
And seld or never doth approche one sleape unto her head.
In stead wherof contrary thoughtes doo occupy her brayne,
And then whole floudes of brokish teares depart from eyes amaine.
Her moystie pilow she doth leave long or the day appeare :
And rechlesly she deckes her selfe, nought forcing what she weare.
Thus clothd, she spends welny the day in temple much devout,
Accompanied with one alone, (and not with glistring rout.
Of Courtlie dames) this Lady hath in charge her booke to beare,
As one that for her parentage the Princes held full deare.   [C2ʳ]
This soone espide Ariodant, that long had sought to finde
Convenient place, and time as fit, to utter out his mynd,
Which seene, welcome the time (he saies) of me desired long :
Wherin I hope to be releast, of this my solom song.
For if I may such frendship finde, of her that beares the booke :
As ones to wayte in stead of her, for more I do not looke.
Then shall my plaint, which written first, and cold in secret wyse :
Within the booke, disclose my care, at full before her eyes.
Wherin she shall perceive also, the fittes of my disease :
And how my cause to her I yeld, to order as shee please.

And if shee be of nature good, though shee disdayne my name :
Yet will shee kepe it secretly, that therby grow no blame.
And if shee hate to rue my care, I know the end of all :
The worst is, that my desperate corpse on goring knife shall fall.
But if she take me to her grace, who lives in better plight :
Or who can vaunt of greater blisse, or is a happier wight? [C2ᵛ]
Thus he concludes and findes out time, and place, and now doth crave :
Of her that daylie beares the booke, the cariage for to have.
The morow, when her Ladie doth to chappell take the way :
Which frienship showe, shall bind me yours for to remaine alway.
(He said). And she yᵗ knew no guile, ne what was his intent,
Except to get the Princes grace, his wilie head was bent.
Which by that means might soone be wonne and then the fruites of
    gayne :
As hopte reward for servitur, in recompence of payne.
As movd with termes of curtesie, doth yeld unto his will :
Who frindly said you have your hest your mind I do fulfill.
Therfore see that to morow next, about the houre of eyght :
You geve attendance in this place, in my steade for to weight.
Ariodant with thousand thankes, requites this freindly graunt :
And voues for her in all assaies, his power shall not want.
Thus part they twoo, the Ladie shee, to Princes grace agayne :
Doth hie : And he, in chamber close doth take no litle payne. [C3ʳ]
In writing out at large, the cause of his longe proved woe,
And when, and where, and how he did, his libertie forgoe.
First how her fame, did force him leave the joyes of native land :
And taught him skale the craggie rock, and saile by fearfull sande.
Then how by soden sight, her shape did steale from him his hart :
Since when, he tels how he hath felt, the paynes of mortall smart.
Herein he makes a long discourse, and ends with answere cravd,
In gentlest wise, that mought have moved, a hart of stone I gravd.
This letter made, & sealed with wax, he hides in secret wise :
And all that night, in steade of sleape, he doth therof devise.
Sometime a lothsome thought, doth bid him leave his rashe intent :
And reason tels him thousand doughtes, his purpose to prevent.
Sometime, he feares least rechlesly, she mought his letter lease :
Or els bewray it to her Syre, his hory head to please.
See here the seede that lovers sowe, wherof doth spring the grayne :
Of doughtfull blisse, that subject is, to drought and stormes of
    rayne. [C3ᵛ]
But feare or shame or dought of death, can nought this lover move :
Though silence if he could have choosd, seemde best for his behove.
And for to move Ariodant, his wylfull path to shunne :
As easie it weare to see the streame, against the tide to runne.

Auroras beames hath banisht night: sir Phebe doth vaunt in East,
Whose plesant hew, rejoyceth byrds and joyes both man, and beast.
Ariodant forsakes his bed, he feares to come to late:
He prayes the happy Mercurie, to send him happy fate.
Now is he come unto the place, where he was warnd to staie:
And thinks long till Jenevora: to Chappell go to pray.
The Princes is attired now, she calleth for her booke:
Wheron she dayly wonted is, in temple for to looke.
The Lady doth present her selfe, before his mistres eyes:
With booke in hand Jenevore, in hast to chappell hyes.
They passe wheres Ariodant doth stand in readines:
To have the promyse now performd which earst I did expresse.   [C4ʳ]
She was as mindefull of her graunt as he of his request:
And therwith gave to him the booke, which she in hand hath prest.
He folowes our Jenevora, she backward doth retire:
His letter in the booke is cold, as he would best desire.
The Princes is come to the pew, wher wonted she doth pray,
He humbly yeld to her the booke, and so departes away.
But when she saw Ariodant, whom more then life she lovd,
(As one amazd) the blushing bloud, from wonted course is movd:
Which drives away the colour pale, which earst was in her face:
(A signe they say of tried truth, and store of giltles grace)
In doughtful plight the Lady kneels if vision she had seene:
Or if conceit of idle brayne, the cause therof had bene.
The truth it selfe doth hardly lodge, within her doutfull head:
Besides the novelties therof, have novell fansies bread.
In these conceites, she opes the booke the letter is descride:
She languisheth till that theffect therof she hath espide.   [C4ᵛ]
With ravish brayn she hath purusd, her lovers dolefull plaint:
And twenty times she doth unread, how love did him attaint.
She reades (with ruth) his termes of grace and eke her answer cravd:
His vowed troth, for ay she reades, which in her hart is gravd.
What shuld I say, the happie newes with auncient woes contend:
So diversly, within her corps, that backward she doth bend.
In sound, as one that lenger had no power to foster life:
Among her vexed limes, (I say) there is such mortall strife.
Thus novel joyes have won the field and banisht woe away:
And gasping life & breathing breath, do helpe to part the fray.
The vanisht bloud retires agayne, the dampishe could is fled,
Assured hope confounds dispayre, and conquers drowsie dred.
Her scorched hart hath moisture found her seared joyntes are strong,
The burning heate, and Isie could, that troubled her so longe.
Are quite exild, and in their steede, the Elements doo rule
Indiffrently, and hastie health, beginnes for to recule.   [C5ʳ]

See here, the wyse Chyrurgion, hath found one salve to cure
His own disease, and hers, that dyd in woe long tyme indure.
Oh happy thryse Ariodant, thy pacient well may say:
When as thy letter hath such grace, to banish cares away.
For as by pearsing looke, eche one, became eche others thrall:
And as by dome of Cupids might, in bondage they did fall:
So by Melpomens sugred style, new freedom eche possest,
He by his letter gaynd that he wuld, and she that pleased her best.
WHen dying fits constraynd by joy, had lost their chokyng force:
And gasping breath, began to rule, in late forsaken corse.
When lyvely bloud, which earst forsoke his wanne and swelling heate:
Had vanquisht death from every part, and pulces fast gan beate:
Then with two streames of joyfull teares, the letter bathed is:
And twyse ten thousand tymes I thinke, the paper she doth kisse.
Now doth she finely close it up, and puttes it next her brest,
Againe unfoulded now it is, now reades she his request.   [C5ᵛ]
She came to Temple much devout, devotion movd hir minde:
But to the Gods, this ravisht dame, in prayers spends small winde.
She rather seekes which way she may behave hir to hir love:
And eke which way, they best may work for both theyr best behove.
She thinkes it sin to deale with him, as some coye Dames doo use:
To feede him with a fayre looke, and after him refuse.
She rather minds, (to ease his care) an answer for to sende:
Wherin like cause, like fits and wo, she myndeth shall be pend.
But least the gasing eye mought vew the secrets of their mynd:
And least theyr lavish letters sent, mought rayse a sclaundrous mynd:
She doth devise a secret meanes how he, without suspect
May easely those letters find, which are to him direct:
And she may have, at that selfe place the answer of hir friend,
And so, eche one may partner be of others faithfull mynde.
With these conceits, the burning chayre doth clyme on hiest heaven,
The Clock agreeth with the Sunne, and sayes it is eleven.   [C6ʳ]
The Lady wayteth by the pewe, and hath three houres large:
Her only prayer is to God, that others [had] her charge.
Thus are her mistres orisons, in order sayd eche one:
Her homeward countnance shows how that, her God hath easd her mone.
Yet modestly her smiling eyes, with sober looke is clad:
She means her mirth wᵗ solom chere although not all so sad.
Thus hath she left yᵉ temples rights, to Court she hies agayne:
She tasted there late lothed meates, she filles with joy her brayne.
The Ladies smile to see this chaunge. the King doth heare this newes,
His heavie hart doth leape for joy, he doth no lenger muse.
But he (poore soule) Ariodant, when he with quaking cheere:
And shaking hand, had geven the booke unto his Lady deere:

His hastie steps do leave the pewe, his prayers soone are donne :
And secretly in chamber he thus hath his tale begonne.
What wants ther now Ariodant? what is ther now behind?
What hard attempt is yet undone? or what is in thy mynd?   [C6ᵛ]
Not yet performd, thou mayst atcheve, and bring unto an ende,
Before the grevous gastly grones, thy wofull hart doth rende.
Behould these eyes of myne, have seene the last of all thy joye :
And this unhappy head to late, doth wayle thy great annoy.
Oh friendles wretch, yᵉ hevens agree, to see thy fatall fall :
And these thy endles dolefull plaints are joye unto them all.
Els, had thy folly never forst thee to attempt this joye :
Which scand, & judged indifferently, deprives thee of thy joy.
Thinkst thou her noble hart can brook thy grosse unegall love :
Who for her shape and semelines, mought match with Gods above.
Thinkst thou, wᵗ patience she can vew the foly of thy brayne :
Whose passing wisdom, wel approvde all earthly wittes doth stayne.
Thinkst thou to scape wᵗout thy hire, of him that rules the land?
Thinkst thou thy wandring letter, found, of all shall not be scand?
Oh witles wretch when steed is stolne, thou seest what may ensue :
But when thou moughst thou couldst not then a present harme
     eschue.   [C7ʳ]
Oh more then thryse unhappy wight, eche open mouth shall sound
To Skies thy shame, when thy vile corpse forgot shall lodge in ground.
Dispatch therfore, why stayes thy hand to geve thy hart his meede :
Whose foolish lust, and fond desire, was causer of this deede.
And therwithall he drew his blade, his desperat part to play :
But reason with hir holsome skyll, forst hastie hand to staie.
Nay rather yeld thou foole (quoth she) to reasons sound advise :
Who greater fits then thou dost feele, can cure with a tryse.
Wilt thou with desperate death deserve, the paynes of lasting smart :
That mayst with eased mynd a whyle finde salve to heale thy hart?
Perchance thy Ladie doth [requite], thy love with love againe :
Why wilt thou then till troth be knowne with dread increase thy payne.
Perchance or this her hart hath felt, for thee lyke fittes and care,
And truth it is, she crased is, and heavely doth fare.
And mait not be that Cupide is a judge indifferent :
Who for taugment your joyes the more, doth thus your lymmes
     torment,   [C7ᵛ]
But love, thou saist, unegall plast is causer of thy care :
(Ah foole) and hast thou now forgot, how Cupide none will spare.
And is not King, and Kayser perst with his artylerie?
And knowst thou not how (blinded) he at ventures lettes it flie?
Canst thou alone then suffer shame, (if shame a man mought call
An honest love, when worlds of men to love are bound and thrall?)

Suppose the King might know thy love, what harme can then insue:
Himselfe or this could hardly shunne, the sparkes of Venus crewe.
Wherfore, let thought be fordest, from the bounds of quiet hart:
And with advise whats best to doe, these passions set apart.
Thy Ladie is a gentill Dame, her bewtie doth declare:
Who for to ease thy greedie minde, an answere will not spare.
Crave once againe the cariage of the booke, thou late didst beare,
And in the cariage search the booke, if ought be lodged there:
Perchaunce as thou didst first invent so she will now devise:
And will her answere ther inclose, thy mynde for to suffise.   [C8ʳ]
These thoughts, (as Phebus clears the skie) from foule infective myst:
Do ease his mynd, & banish thought, out from his cloudy brest.
In western seas swift Phaeton, doth plunge his gleaming chayre,
And in his steed the gliding starres, doth compasse loftie ayre.
When in his bed Ariodant doth couch his heavy head:
In hope to sleape but fansies newe, doo rule in [Sopors] stead.
The Princes is to closet gone not rekles of her friend,
And least her deeds mought be espide, the dore is lockt and pynd.
Then takes she paper, pen, and Ink, and thus writes to her own:
Take this (not as an answere sent) from one to thee unknown.
But let these lines be guide to thee, which way thou mayst attayne,
Unto my answer, craved that doth, by Olive tree remaine.
Repayre therfore Ariodant, to privie gardayn where:
Under the mightie Olive tree, by me lies hidden there.
That thou didst crave, this may suffise, at full thy longing minde:
Till more at large, at fitter time, thou shalt my answer finde.   [C8ᵛ]
(This done) she takes an other shete of paper, which doth serve:
To answere to his letter sent, for which he nie doth sterve.
Therin she blisseth thryse the tyme when he did tread on ground:
Of Scottish Realme, whose like (quoth she) in earth can not be found.
Therin she blisseth eke him selfe, that would take such great payne:
To see so meane a wight as she, in whom doth not remayne.
Halfe that great prayse, which he bestowes, on her unworthy shape:
Which is the worst that ever did, from natures handes escape.
Then dolefully she doth lament, his long sustained woe:
His pining fittes, unquiet rest, his cares she rues also.
Now is the time, when Venus first did thrall her to her lore:
Declared eke, and care, for care, she doth requite, and more.
Now doth she, (like an Oratres) perswade him to be true:
She vows by Jove to shun the paths, that she wils him eschue.
What should I say, she tels yᵉ time, she tels the secret place:
When either, other person, may without suspect imbrace.   [D1ʳ]
Untill which time, she wished him, amendment of his fittes:
With thousand joyes, which to declare, would trouble sore my wittes.

Well wery hand and watched eye, seeke now longe shunned rest:
As sleape to work thy drousie charme, at hand is ready prest.
This night, the glad Jenevora, of sleape receiveth more:
Then in six months and odde (I think) she did receive before.
Ariodant (as Marchant tost with stormes from kenned land:
That feares by rock, or swallowing goulfe, his deaths day is at hand)
Dispayring lies, and dreadfull thoughtes oppresse his crased minde:
And doughting most that battred barke, so soone good port should finde.
Yet as he had concluded, he by breake of day doth ryse:
And in dispite of fortune, mindes tachiefe his interpryse.
Jenevora, (though heavy head, did crave more golden sleape,)
Is not unmindfull of her charge: ne lenger bedde doth keape.
But long before Ariodant, she doth unknown arise:
And with her letter hastely, to privie garden hies.   [D1^v]
And as she had devised earst, within her little scrowle:
She hides it by the Olive tree, unknown to any soule.
That done, to warme an easie bed (not waking any wight,)
She plies againe, and lieth till Aurora geveth light.
Then up she startes, & decks her self, with costlie robes of gould:
Her glistring hear, in sumptuous cal the courtly Dames doo fould.
Then close in closet she doth put the scrowle into the booke:
Which first she made, of purpose, y^t her friend theron should looke.
That done, she thus commaundes her mayd, if he doth come this day:
That last did beare the booke, when I, to chappell went to pray.
And crave the booke agayne of you, [graunte] him (quoth she) his
    mynd,
The straunger shows a courtiers part it comes from gentill minde.
With dutie done, the Lady graunts, unto her Ladies will:
That in her stead doth wish he had, of wayting full his fill.
Ariodant, abideth nowe, in his appointed place:
But fearfulnes compels him hyde, his blushing, bashfull face.   [D2^r]
Till that the Princes past the place, where lurking he did stay:
She is scarce gone, when secretly, the Lady he doth pray.
Once more in steede of her to wayte, and cariage for to have:
Of prayer booke, she graunts it him, he hath that he did crave.
Then secretly the fearfull man, doth prie within the booke:
The scrowle he finds, & takes it out, he cannot therin looke.
For fervent joye: he puts it up, she is now come to pewe:
He geves ye booke with blushing face, his Lady that doth vewe.
Her smiling chere, bids him farwell: his hastie foote doth part:
These frendly looks, which after that for ever lodge in hart.
This longing lover is aryvd, at chamber, now in hast:
He opes ye scrowle, & word for word, he findes in order plast.
As erst I [tould]: he heves his handes, and streacht out armes to skies:

His clothes he bathes with gushing teares, that run from swelling eyes.
His joye is in her secretnes, that myndes not to disclose:
His proferd love, as by thappointed place he doth suppose.   [D2ᵛ]
For though (quoth he) the answere be not as my fansie would:
Yet by this meanes to show my mynd, no doubt I may be bould.
And though she now doth light esteeme, and will not heare my plaint:
In tract of time my fittes I trust, her stony hart may taint.
For rust in tyme, will canker in the gad of sturdy steele:
And littel worme in tract of tyme, doth make the Oke to reele.
In time, by droppes of raynie dew, the firie flint doth freat:
In time also the beating sea, the ruggie rock doth eate.
And may not then in time my sobbes and teares, from drowned eyes:
Pearse gentil hart, whose nature is, to rule on wofull cryes?
Besids if lookes may move me think my love she doth requite:
I neede no greater proofe then that wherof I late had sight.
For did not colour chaunge in face, when she beheld me fast:
First read as any Rose in May, and pale agayne at last?
Some say that these be arguments, of vext, and troubled minde:
And sonest seene in lovers face: (as I in writers finde.)   [D3ʳ]
But why doo I thus spend the time, in dought, and doughtfull toyes:
When answer seen and once perusd, may ease perhaps annoyes.
And therwithall, like greedy wolfe, nye sterved for his pray:
He leaves his talke and hastelie to gardin takes the way.
Where prively, at bidden place, he seekes with curious eyes:
The answer which his Ladie did, for him of late devyse.
The joyfull man hath found it out, his labour now is don:
He leaves the gardin for that nyght, he doth to lodging runne.
Wher carefully, he doth unfould, the letter closlie seald:
And readeth eke by surcamstance, that was by dreame reveald.
And (as I sayd) how she extolles, his shape unto the skyes:
And how of her renoumed grace, she basely can devise.
Then how she rewes yᵉ scorching fits which he so long hath felt:
And then as touching her ill rest how love with her hath delt.
Next that, her wyse perswasion he with leaping hart doth reede:
Then fixed faith and plighted troath, till death doth crave his
    meed.
                                                                   [D3ᵛ]
Oh happy newes, oh joyfull lines, oh sentence glad pronounst:
That makes him seke for ravisht wits, that so in cares wast trounst.
Come helpe ye Mountain Ladies al, and leave Pernassus hill:
Come help me with your sugred stile my charge for to fulfill.
And thou, oh Spring of eloquence, come helpe to guyde my hand:
That rudely doth presume to write, in verse but grosly scand:
Of joyes, that had their ginning first of black and lothsome fittes:
Come helpe therfore Apollo thou, to wheat my dulled wittes.

And help oh knights of Cupids crew on whom dame Venus smiles:
To write of blisse, and more then joye, that floudes of cares exiles.
For your report must make my skill by proufe I nought can write:
Of joyes, although (ye more my ruth) of cares I can indight.
But sith the listing eare doth wayte, to heare howe he doth fare:
That late receivd these gladsome newes such wynde I now will spare.
And sith both Musis, Gods, and Men, disdayne to rue my plaint:
You must w^t baser verse, (my lords) your learned heads acquaint. [D4^r]
Therfore, when hungrie eyes had fed long tyme on pleasant newes:
And gladnes bad his pining corse, such mourning to refuse.
With bowed knee, his joyned handes, to hautie heaven he houldes:
And then unto the mightie Jove, he thus his mynd unfouldes.
Perpetuall prayse immortall God, (that all of nought didst frame)
Be dewe to thee, and lasting grace, be geven unto thy name:
That from the toppe of hiest heaven to deepest vale belowe:
Dost (like a gentell Savior,) on me such pitie showe.
Whose sinfull deeds, doo dayly move, thy godly mynde to yre:
And parchase eke, (by just desert,) the paynes of dreadfull fyre.
Thy goodnes (Lord) no tong can tell, ne head can well devise:
No pen can paint such worthy prayse, as may thy deede suffise.
My hart unable is to think, thy goodnes showd to mee:
That w^t thy might, hast socourd one, quite drownd in miserie.
For was not I the wofulst wretch, that lived under skyes:
Consumd with care, nye chockt with sobbes, besprent with teares, and
    cryes. [D4^v]
And now, who lives in greater blisse who now more happier wight,
Whose fate doth fortune favor more, or who in better plight?
Wherfore, if thou (oh mightie Jove) wilt bryng to happie end,
This love begonne, which in thy law we mind till death to spend:
If thou (I say) (as thou dost knowe, the secrets of my hart,
Be quite from guyle, & fardest from the sinne that asketh smart:)
Wilt turne our former passions of vile consuming care,
To lasting joye, and perfect blisse, and graunt to us, the share
Of spousals rights, which more then goods, or friends, or life I love,
I vow, by all that earst thou framdst in earth, and heaven above,
By this my soule I vow, I sweare, I firmly doo protest,
To love, to dread, and serve thee lord whylst lyfe lodge in my brest.
This vow he made, and up he starts, he feeles he thinks no ground:
His limmes that earst for weaknes bowd, in strength do now abound.
His mynde runnes on Jenevora, and of hir worthy hew,
He gives to hir the chiefest prayse, of all fayre bewties crewe. [D5^r]
He thinkes now of the courteous lines, whiche she to him did sende:
He reades them till by hart eche worde he knowes, and then doth rende
The paper, least by some mishappe, the letter lost and founde:

Mought turne to his decaye, and hers, to whome he chiefe is bounde.
Now thinkes he of the joyfull place, whiche she did late invent:
Where he with sight of her his joye, his minde he mought content.
Against which time he deckes himselfe with sutes of joyfull hewe,
And throwes away his mournyng weedes, he lothes on them to vewe.
He now doth vaunt him self, amongst the rout of courtly mates:
His gladnes, hath brought hunger to, he feedes on costly cates
He is not now on tomblyng bed, nor wandryng nowe alone:
He doth not nightly now lament, nor filles the skies with mone:
But like a careles youth the daye, in sundrie sportes he spendes,
And so the nightes in maskes, and showes, he bringeth to their endes
In fine, eche care, that whylom was, to him griefe and annoie:
Is nowe become a treble blisse, and twentie fould more joye.   [D5ᵛ]
Then if he earst had never felt, of woe the cutting fittes,
Or if the stormes of lothsome love had never tost his wittes.
His brother, (that was partner long of his unquiet rest)
Is glad with him, & drives forth with vyle care from carefull brest.
His mind, (yᵗ earst was dulled quite) his lyms, (that lothed disport)
Is wakt from dreame, and now he is as stiffe as mightie fort.
Now wants he nought but mates to stande, the dint of his great speare:
Or such as would in open field, against him armour beare
But none there are in Scottish soyle no none that beareth life:
(That knowes his might) that dare advance him selfe before his knife.
Therfore, in stede of justes on hors, and tourneis done on foote,
In forest wyde, the savage beast, in dennes he seeketh out,
Wherby the countrey man doth live at home in suertie:
And keepes therby him selfe, and his, from former jeoperdie.
But why do I of profit speake, wher pleasure is my song?
Or what hath Bloudie Mars to doo, amongst Cupidos throng?   [D6ʳ]
Why sayst thou pen, to speak of him that armed is with joy:
And prest against fayre Ladies foes, his might for to imploy?
Why telst thou not how he hath now disclosed to his love,
(In presence) all his former woes, (which hard) forthwith do move
The Cristal drops from smilyng eyes by streames for to discend:
She showes like fittes, which forse from hart the broken sighes tassend.
Then he with foulded armes imbrast her small and semely wast:
And she her slender joynts, about her lovers neck hath cast.
A thousand tymes he kissed hath her lippes of rosiat hew.
As oft she doth unkisse againe, her friend and lover trew.
Now doth his tongue confirme those fittes, which penne did late indight:
As how with sighes the day he spent and with lyke teares the night.
Then how with hope he was alurd, to sue for wyshed grace:
And how in dream with goddesse two he saw her heavenly face.
The princes hears, this plesant talke and then she did unfould,

What sightes, what shapes, and visions, she in night tyme did be-
    hould.   [D6ᵛ]
With such like talke, the tyme is spent, and now is come the howre :
When sugrie presence, they must change for pensife parting sowre.
They rue their want, and hate the tyme, that byds them to depart :
But needes they must, though corsie strong, it is for them to start.
He geves in signe of loyal love unto the Princes grace,
A Diamond of passing prise, a ringe that did abace :
All Juels that before that tyme, were seene in Scottish land :
Whose gleming stone causd gasing eyes on musing oft to stand.
She takes the ring with joyful hart, she geves to him againe
A token, which doth signifie, she faithfull will remaine.
With joyned lips, they say farewell, with pressed hand in hand
They vow : that to that place ech day to come no let shall stand.
Againe they kisse, and faintly then, mine own adew (quoth he)
With becked hand, and bowed head, my heart farewell (quoth she)
Their backward lookes show loth to part, theyr hartes agree also :
That to enjoy eche others sight : great wealth they would forgo.   [D7ʳ]
Thus are they come, she to the court, among the glistring rout
Of chast Dianas nimphes, and he repayres, amongst the stout
And sturdy band, of Scottish knights where he doth passe the daye,
In decent games, in courtly sportes, and other seemely playe.
Sometime with racket he doth tosse the light reboundyng ball,
And carfully doth marke the chase : now he his hauke doth call :
And now his barbed horse he traynes to passe his swift carear :
· Or els to gallope round the field, now doth he with his speare,
By steadie [course] obteyne the ryng, and now by forsed mighte,
He breaks his staffe, & now he learns his carvyng [glayve] to byte
On forged sheld (That done) on foote he runnes a breathyng race,
And then returnes to court to wayt, before his Lieges grace :
Which he can doo in seemeliest sort, therin he hath such skill :
That better then the best he doth, his courtly charge fulfill
The dyner don, he filles his eares, with heavenly melodie,
And he him selfe on solom lute, can stryke sweete hermonie.   [D7ᵛ]
And now amongst the Scottishe Dames, (as though he weare to chuse)
He would discourse of histories, and tell of forein newes.
As first the siege of worthy Troy, what knightes therin weare slayn :
And how that Helen was the cause, that Grecians felt such paine.
Then how, the chast Penelope, did leade a widowes lyfe :
Til hir Ulix, and Anthenor, did ende the tenne yeares strife.
Next how Eneas, falsly delt, with Dido, Carthage Queene,
And how for falsing of her faith, False Creseide fell uncleane.
A thousand such this curious knight reports unto this crew,
And all (god knows [ ]), was to the end his Ladie for to vewe.

The Courtiers they delight to heare his passing eloquence,
They thank him al, he seeks no more he hath his recompence.
He is (good soule) a happie man, that by that meanes he may :
At pleasure and without suspect, see his Jenevora,
Amongst these jestes, he mindfull is, of secrete meetyng place :
He cannot that forget, where he his Lady shall imbrace.   [D8ʳ]
There (as it lighted in his head) he doth unloode his brayne,
And she, as amours forse her speake, doth yeld the like againe.
Their other passions I commit to you that lovers be :
I cannot think, much lesse to wryte, theyr fittes of jolytie.
But many daies these faithfull ones did spend in great delight :
And lenger had, if fortune had, not wrought them great dispit :
For whilst they two with quiet myndes had driven away the cloude
Of carefulnes, and nought but blisse, within their harts did shrowd,
(I faint to tell) that Serpent vile, that worketh Princes woe :
That treason black, forst them (alas) theyr freedom to forgoe.
Therfore, a dew, without desert, ye Nymphes of Helicon :
Possesse your Mount I need you not let my rude verse alone.
Tis Sibil she that Profitesse : that knowes, the darksome denne
Of Plutos Realm, that must be ayde to guyde my rugged penne.
We must amongst the lothsome shades, seeke out Alecto vile :
That may with mone, and solome tune, deck this my dolefull style. [D8ᵛ]
Thou Jove graunt that I may finde out, The bough of golden
     hewe :
And that the teeth of hellish dogge, I safely may eschewe.
And thou (I say) that worker art, of this my changed songe :
Help with thy Snakie hears to show the sting of treason strong.
For thou, thou Witch, thou hellish hagge, thou wrinkled fury fell,
Hast forst my pen that painted blisse, of foule mishappe to tell.
But sith with scorched limmes he craves, to [write] his cruell fall :
Whom fortune late with honour deckt, and reard to noble wall.
I will assay to turne my stile, from lovers happy life :
To frowning fittes, to sobbes, to cryes, to falshod cause of strife :
And sith he seekes to have his fall, a myrrour to the rest :
That [live] I will begin with him, and let the other rest.
THere was amongst the Scottish Lordes, (whom honour did advaunce
To noble style,) a mightie Duke, of bloud, although hard chaunce,
Oh filthie facte, dispoyld him quite of former dignitie :
And forst him leave his tipe of might, to perverse miserie.   [E1ʳ]
This Prince was Duke of Albany, and Pollinesso hight :
And vassall to the Scottish king, a subtill craftie knight.
Who well increast in aged yeeres, (and yet to chuse a feare)
Gan greatly love Jenevora, whom he as live helde deare.
And sith he was of noblest birth, of subjectes in the land :

He thought shee rather to obtayne, that he did take in hand.
Wherfore he is in mynd oft tymes, to move the King herein:
Whose grace once got, he soner thinks the Princes for to win.
Againe thinks he, if she should know my mynd is for to crave:
Her fathers graunt, before I doo her favour seeke to have:
The stately dame perhaps wold dain my sute and profred love:
Therfore he minds this way to deale as for his best behove,
He seekes (I say) to spend the tyme, with her in stately court:
To play with her at chesse, or cardes, or other chamber sport.
And when he sees she pleasant is, and in her mery vayne:
To breake to her such amours, as within his hart remaine.   [E1ᵛ]
So thought, so don, he wears the day as earst he did devise:
He hath his fill of Ladies lookes, he feades therwith his eyes.
But see the spight that jelousie that prieth every where,
Hath brought him in an agonie, and in a soden feare.
He sees the straunger [oft] resort, to his rejoysing place:
He sees his Ladie showes to him a pleasant smiling face.
But most of all, and that that most augmentes his jelousie:
Is straungers ring, which she doth weare, still gleaming in his eye.
Wherwith, dispayring in his mynde of his late hoped gayne:
He thinks to spend more time therin is booteles and in vayne.
Yet doth affection tell him that his doughtes be contrarie:
The Straunger cometh to the court (saith he) of curtesie.
And she requireth, like, for like, what if she weare his Ring?
The stone is rich, and happely, she hath therin liking.
Besides, will she bestowe her love of one a straunger borne:
Of mean estate? when Princes loves she oft hath had in scorne?   [E2ʳ]
Thus hope, and dought doo hould this Duke, he long hath felt what payne:
Dispayre doth bring, and eke what toyes, in doughtfull fittes remayne.
And when he sawe that wearing tyme, could nothing wast his dought:
Inforst by love and jelousie, this fetch he hath found out.
Firstly, for to acquaint him self, with this Ariodant:
That dayly doth (as well as he) to Princes lodging haunt.
And then, for to invite him home, unto his mancion:
Where he concludes to put in use, this last invention.
That is, to hauke and hunt with him, and passe the time away:
In such disportes as he delightes, chiefly to weare the day.
In which meane time he wil disclose the secretes of his mynde:
To him, as both his owne affaires, and such as are assingde.
By privie counsell, for the wealth, of all the Scottish lande:
And eke what actes the king intends, with speede to take in hand.
Then of his private deedes to tell, and how he leades his life:
And eke with whom he is in leage, and eke with whom in strife.   [E2ᵛ]
Al these & more then these, this Duke doth mynd for to disclose:

To his invited gest at home, only of this purpose.
To have the straunger yeld agayne, the secrets of his hart:
In recompence of that which he, to him did late impart.
Amongst which things, he hopes to heer of this suspected love:
And so to be resolvd of that, which jelousie did move.
And if it be (as he suspect) (I meane) that she hath chusde
Ariodant unto her fere, and he hath eke refusde.
All other for Jenevora, then he in friendly wyse,
Will beat into the straungers head, what harmes therof may ryse.
Or els to perswade him that, his time is spent in vayne:
In suing to obtayne her grace, that doth great Lordes disdayne.
And how, that she doth mynd disceit, and nought esteemes his love:
As Ladie wilie heades doo oft, the sielie soule to prove.
With such conceites as these, the Duke doth thinke for to beguile:
This careles man, that falshods craft, hath fardest in exile.   [E3ʳ]
And now, from craftie Parlament, he calles his wylie wittes:
In mynde, in hast to put in use this same, to ease his fittes.
And finding now Ariodant amongst the courtly crewe:
Of Scottish Dames, yᵗ joyes in hart his Lady for to vewe.
He doth acquaint him self with him and with a friendly face:
Invites him to his stately home, and courtly dwelling place.
The straunger (that for courtesie excells the Scottish rout)
(Whose giltles mind culd not devise this treason to search out)
With bowed knee, and humble thanks requites his jentlenes:
And shows himself at his commaund as prest in readines.
The Duke is glad, that thus he hath achevd his interpryse:
The straunger joyes, & hopes hereby some happy happe may rise.
Now both have left yᵉ Regall court, both leave their Ladies sight:
And now amidst the plesaunt fieldes to sport doo both delight.
Sometime their running feete pursue the cry of yelling hounde:
Sometime they joy to smite the deare or els the hart to wound.   [E3ᵛ]
Sometime in arms, they seke yᵉ chase of Beare or Lyon fearce:
Or els with sharp and cutting glayve the tusked Boare to pearce.
When day is gon, they welcom night with showes and harmonie:
Or els with well squard champions, to force their treasure flie.
Amongst these sports & plesant jests the Dukes let not to tel:
What diverse haps have chaunst to him, and all that earst befell
As well to him, as to the Realme, he telles to him the state:
Of all the soyle, and Region: besides he doth dilate.
What is agreed, by close consent, of all the Scottish peares:
And then what lawes are ordained, he beates into his eares.
Then how in youth he trapped was, with traynes of Cupides might:
(He tels) and how unhappie man, he servde a scornefull wight.
Since when, (he saies,) how he hath lothd such passions to sustaine:

The fruit wherof wil not (quoth he) halfe countervayle the payne.
Ariodant, with listing eare, markes well this diverse talke
And takes good heede unto his tale, when lavish tounge doth
   walke.   [E4^r]
But from his lippes doo not proceede the secretes of his hart :
Ne from his close, and privie mynd no passed actes depart.
He countes it vilanie to tell, that he could well declare :
And taught he was from infancie, a walking tongue to spare.
Therfore unto him selfe he keepes, that lodgeth in his mynde :
And stayes his mouth from breathing out his thoughts unto the wynde.
Wherwith the Duke, not well content, but moved much with ire :
(Considring that it fell not out as he did earst desire)
(With angry cheere) Unkind (quoth he) is this the curtesie
That you unkind Italians, requite for amitie.
How can thy greedy eares keepe in, such store of secrets tould :
Without imparting lyke for lyke, and not for to unfould.
Such jestes as hidden lye in brest, which may content my mynd :
And ease perhappes a troubled head, as therby friendes oft finde.
This said, & hard, with blushing face, the straunger as dismayde :
With fixed looke, and sober chere, unto the Duke thus sayd.   [E4^v]
I trust my Lord your honour will not so accompt (quoth he)
Of him that doth remayne as yours, and is from falshood free.
For we that be of Italie, and borne in foren lande :
Doo think it mearest vanitie, and fond to take in hand.
To treat of that, that profit smal redoundes to them that heare
The same, and most of all, in vayne, that goulden tyme doth weare.
To hould your honor with such acts, as I my youth did spend
In Italie (my native soyle) to small effect would tende.
Sith both the land to you unknown, the deedes of such purporte :
As heard & judgd, your self would say doo not discerve report
And since my wandring feete did leve the bounds of Italie,
No acte hath past from me that hath, deserved memorie.
Therfore (w^t pardon cravd my Lord) I trust you will esteeme,
But well of this my silent tongue, and rightly therof deeme.
(Quoth he) and then began the Duke no, no, Ariodant,
Thy deedes are not so secret done, ne yet my wittes so scant.   [E5^r]
But well I can behould the thing, that thou doest shunne to saie :
Both how thou hast and lovest now, the Prince Jenevora.
Thy oft resort unto hir court, discloseth thy intent :
Thy plesant lookes to her doo show, thy wyll therto is bent.
But if thy reckles head had wayde, my good wyll borne to thee :
Thou wuldst not once have stickt to tell, those secrets unto mee.
Whose sage advise perhaps mought move, thy mynde from that intent :
Which yelds in fine nought els but sighes, and cares for tyme so spent.

Yet sith at first, my fansie had, in thee so good thinking,
I will inforce my tounge to speake, against my lustes lyking:
Know thou therfore, (Ariodant) the Princesse hates thy love,
And scornes that thou should so presume, therto her grace to move.
For though with smyling chere she doth, reward thy curtesie:
Yet is her mynde most fardest from, the lustes of Venorie:
Beleve well, Ariodant, thy love is evill imployde,
For I it is, whom she doth love, whose hart I have injoyde.   [E5ᵛ]
Long time, of whom I may commaund, what listeth me to crave,
And eke obteyne what so I aske, as proved oft I have.
And least thy doughtfull head mought deme untroth in this my tale:
I wyll (to put thee out of dought) this enterpryse assaile:
That is, to bring the morow next, from my Jenevora:
Thy Dyamond, thy gift to her the rynge (that men doo say)
In clearnes shames our Scottishe gemmes, wherby, thou mayst perceyve,
How well of thee, and of thy love, thy Lady doth conceyve.
This tale, no soner enterd had into the straungers eare:
But therwithal a heape of thoughts, within his minde appeare.
Yet least his chaunged countnance mought bewray his secrete care:
And least his stayed speach mought showe, how he ny chokt doth fare:
With strained voyce, & moved minde, he firmly doth denie,
Eche point of his accusing tale, and profers for to die,
If ever so his mynd was bent, or if he sought to move
At any tyme the Princes grace, with his unegall love.   [E6ʳ]
And as unto his oft repayre, unto her graces Court:
Shows nought (quoth he) but youthful mynd with Ladies for to sport.
As courtiers use, (of lustie age,) to weare the time away,
In daunce, in talke, in melodie, and other chamber play.
But all for nought, Ariodant his tounge & speach doth spend,
His vowes are vowed all in vayne, the Duke hates to attende
Unto his long excusing tale, and how he doth denie
The gift of that rich Diamond, which he did late discrie.
Wherfore the Duke in hast departs, and doth commaund beside,
His steede for to be sadled straight, for he post hast wyll ryde.
Thus leaves he poore Ariodant, and he to court doth hie,
And (as he rydes) he studies how this Ring he might come by.
At last, he doth record, how that there serves the princes grace
A Ladie that Dalinda hight, a mayde of Scottish race.
Who earst was proferd to the Duke in lawfull mariage:
A seemely wyght, a Lady fayre, of noble parentage.   [E6ᵛ]
But he, nought forsed then the mayd his hautie hart was bent:
With hier match, & greater sums, his wil for to content.
To this forsaken Dame, this Duke concludeth for to goe,
To crave, by proferd mariage, the Dyamond also.

And as he ended had the thoughtes, of this subtill minde :
He is arived at the court, where he doth seeke to finde
In secret wyse, this wayting mayde, whome he at last hath founde
Disporting her, with Lute alone low set upon the ground.
Her he salutes as tyme did serve and she requites againe
His courtesie, that done, the Duke still mindfull of his payne :
Doth crave a word in secreat with the Lady for to have :
And she that least suspects disceite doth graunt that he doth crave.
And then the Duke with sober chere, unlodes his charged mynde
Thus, to the listning maid that longs to heare of newes by kynde.
To hould thee long mine own (qd he) with painted tedious talk,
Or els, in glosing eloquence, to strayne my tounge to walke.   [E7ʳ]
I seeke not now, but simply, I the secretes of my hart :
As playne, as of a perfect truth, to thee I wyll impart.
Thou knowst (qd he) not long or this thy faithfull friendes did move,
(By reason good and great advise) me greatly to thy love :
Thou knowst (I think) also the cause that forst me not consent :
I meane, thy welth, and parentage, could not my mynde content.
For I (as thou doest know right wel) (without bost be it spoke)
For noble lyne, and lyving great, mought match with Royall stocke.
But leavyng thus these lofty lettes inforst through hautie mynde :
And speakyng to affections force, that conquers all by kynde.
Know thou, since then recording oft, those vertuous giftes of thyne :
And eke thy beutie great, which doth excell before myne eyne :
Forgettinge eke, the causes all, of that my former staye :
And callyng now unto my mynde, thy woorthy shape, I saye,
I am as ready now to yelde, unto [thy] friendes desire :
As they to gayne my graunt, or this, were willyng to require.   [E7ᵛ]
And sith, it is unknown to me, which way thy wyll is bent :
And eke for proufe how willingly, thou doest therto consent :
If thou wilt not deny me that, which I of thee will crave :
Which thou at ease maist graunt, I seeke, no greater proufe to have.
That is, when our Jenevora, in bed doth take her rest :
And when the slumbryng sleape doth rule, within her quiet brest :
To helpe me to the Dyamond which she esteemes so wel.
(I meane) the straungers rynge that dooth, in clearnes so excell.
If this to doo, thou wilt not let, by knighthoods lore (I sweare)
To wed thee as my lawfull wife, and I to dye thy feare.
He sayd, and endeth so his tale, and she (when long in muse
Had stayde) in pleasant wise [these] woords or lyke them thus did use.
If this proceede, my Lord (qd she) from bounds of spotles mynde,
And if your proferd curtesie, agree to noble kinde :
If that the secrets of your hart, be voyde of hidden guyle :
And deepe deceit in this your tale, be fardest in exile.   [E8ʳ]

Though dutie biddes me staie to graunt, unto your hastie will :
And reason sayes, with honour I cannot your heste fulfill :
Yet to perswade your honour, that I prest am to obey :
To what so listeth you demaund I will without delay,
Inforse my selfe against the grounds, of bounden duties lore :
To helpe you to the Dyamond, or els to die therfore.
Tyll then a whyle my Lord (qd she) staie you at this selfe place,
And I will to Jenevora, and wayte before her grace,
Till that to sleape she geves hir selfe, and then I will againe
Repaire to you, with Diamond, if here you will remayne.
The Duke agrees to her devise, and (with a joyfull hart :)
Doth yelde to hir a thousand thanks : Dalinda doth depart,
And leaves the Duke wel easd of care and now in perfect blisse :
Because he hopes the straunger will, dispayre at sight of this.
The quiet tyme that nature yeldes, unto the loden mynd
Is come, and now the weary bones, a resting place doo finde.   [E8ᵛ]
Jenevora, (when bankettes all, and revell routes weare done)
Repayres unto her quiet bedde, and watching crewe doth shunne.
Dalinda waites on her this night, of purpose to obtaine
The Diamond, which nightly did on chamber boorde remayne.
Jenevora no sooner had on pillow coucht her head :
But Ring Dalinda fingerd hath, of Diamond she is spead :
And (duty done) the stately couch, she leaveth for that night :
And to Duke Polinesse then, she guydes her feete aright.
Who found in place appointed, she presentes before his eyes.
The Jem, & therwithall, these words she spendeth in this wyse.
As, to content your doughtfull mind my might I have imployde :
And as in you my honour staies, which earst my self injoyde.
So let me finde (my Lord) agayne, in gage of willing hart :
Like deeds unto those vowed words, which late from you did part.
She sayd, and then, the Duke replies thus to her just request.
Or els (qd. he) thou God graunt that no life lodge in my brest.   [F1ʳ]
In signe wherof, hold here (quoth he) and so they joyned handes :
Let this conclude till fitter time the yoke of wedded bandes :
Thus he departs, with promise made before the breake of day :
To yeld againe the Dyamond, no let at all should staye.
Now is the Duke returned safe, unto his heavy gest :
Who long hath lurkt on weary bed, berevd of former rest.
So much this late unlookt for tale, dismayes his quiet hart :
That now well nye he feeles againe, her former woe and smart.
The Duke no sooner leaves his steed but to Ariodant
He hies : that seemes to be a sleape, though ease in head is scant.
And with a pleasant voyce he sayes, what sluggard how, awake :
Thou dreamst to long : from closed eyes the misty sleape of shake.

With that, the straunger (as gest) doth cast his heavy head :
Aloft, and start well nye from out, his tost and tomled bed.
And therwithal, what newes (qd he) who calles me thus in hast :
How fares my lord yᵉ Duke his grace and then his armes he caste. [F 1ᵛ]
Out of the bed, in mynde to ryse, but then Duke Polinesse
Gan name him self, and thus to him these wordes he did expresse.
Let not my hasty call, molest thy head late easd of care :
Ne think no harm, in that (quoth he) thus bouldly I do fare.
For as I have bene grief to thee by breaking of thy sleape :
So may I profit bring to thee, if thou good heede wilt keape.
Unto this tale, which from the hart of him, that wisheth well :
To thee proceedes that found out thy present cares texpell.
I trust thou doughtest not (quoth he) of this my zealous minde :
Which since our first acquaintaunce, hath to helpe thee ben inclinde.
Since when thou knowst, by long discours, what talke hath past from
    mee :
As touching these affections fond, which I conceivd in thee.
At which self time, though thou dist scorne, to tell me what I knew :
Yet did I friendly promise thee, to helpe thee to eschewe.
Those happes, to bring from court with me thy famous Diamond :
Whose match cannot compared be in this our Scottish ground.   [F2ʳ]
Therby, that thou moughtst plainly see, what love in Ladies lookes :
And that in time thou moughst be taught, to shun their hidden hookes.
To quite my self to thee, therfore, of faithfull promise made :
And of my troth unfaind to thee, thy mynd for to perswade.
See heere (& therwith showd the Ring which he in purse did beare)
Beleve thy selfe, not me, if that thy Lady houldes the deare.
When al was said, & Ring was showd and Duke had done his fill :
For to perswade Ariodant, to bridell reckles will.
When in a muse the straunger had, a little whyle remaynde :
Set straight upon his quiet bed, him selfe to speake thus strainde.
The curtesie which I have found in this your graces court :
Hath bounde me till my fatall day, (my Lord) for to report.
Immortall prayses of your grace, to whom I doo account :
My selfe as farre [indetted] to, as my rude head can count.
And sith eche way I see my self, unable to requite :
Your least and smalest benefite, (the more my griefe and spite)   [F2ᵛ]
Yet count me as your own (qd. he) your vassall to commaund :
As one whose life, & goods are yours till death his due demaund.
My duty, thus acknowledged, let these replie unto :
Your graces tale, which in my mynd I well have wayd also.
I doo record right well, (my Lord) the summe of all (quoth he)
As of the Princes grace, what talke past then twixt you and me.
I mindfull am besides, what I spake in myne own defence :

What oths past eke from me to prove my troth, or you went hence.
But that culd not suffice your mynd ne change your wrong intent:
But needs you would (the rather to inforce me to consent.
To that my giltles conscience lothd) to court in hast to hye:
To bring from thence, a Diamond, which, then she said, that I,
Did geve unto Jenevora, therby that I mought see
What good account of you she makes, and how she deales with me.
This was the very talke it self, except I doo forget:
The sum of that within mine eares, is ringing still as yet.   [F3ʳ]
To which, more then I answerd earst I cannot now replie:
But as I sayd, so I protest the same not to denie.
And as unto the remnant of your last pronounced tale:
This shall suffice, if in your hart, my truth may ought avayle.
Know you, (my Lord) I do confesse, the Princes scorneth mee:
For why, a simple courtier I, and meanest in degree.
Not worthy to be thought upon, in Princes hauty court:
Whose birth unknown, doth rather seeke with meaner match to sport.
And as I doo confesse the one, so firmely I denie:
That earst I never sawe this gemme, that thus shines in myne eye.
Nor never gave the like to her, as I am subject true:
Unto my liege and soveraigne, and owe him service due.
Thus I conclude, in hope also, as I have plainly toulde:
The hidden secrets of my hart, and as I have unfould.
Nought els but truth, as you may trie, in time to come right well:
That so you will from doughtfull mynde, such straunge conceites
      expell.
                                                                      [F3ᵛ]
The Duke, (that heares with grief the ende of this late coyned tale)
Amazed stands, sith his intent, no better did prevaile.
Yet minds he, sith the straunger was to him but as a gest:
Not ferder to examine him, but for to let it rest.
Till that at fitter time, he may a better way invent:
For to annoy Ariodant, and eke him selfe content.
And, therwithall, would God (qd he) I wish for thy behove:
That as thou saist, so tract of time, the truth herein may prove.
And parting thence, good night (qd he) take now thy quiet rest:
And to your grace, god graunt (qd he) such ease as likes you best.
Thus is Duke Polinesso come, unto his chamber, where
Unto a secrete friend of his he geves the ring, to beare.
Unto his friend Dalinda, least, the Diamond shuld be wanting:
And so prevent his purpose, and turne to her great undoing.
Post hast, therfore this messenger, is prekt with Diamond
To court, who at the last, by happe Dalinda hath out found.   [F4ʳ]
To whom, (with thousand thankes) he geves the gleaming gem agayne:
From Polinesso (mighty Duke) that doth her friend remayne.

Thus leave I him that ended hath his message in best wise:
And now unto Ariodant, I will my stile devise.
When Polinesso uttred had, that lurked in his brest:
And showed had the Diamond, unto his heavy gest.
When gon he was out of the sight, of poore Ariodant:
Who in his new disquiet mynde ould corsies did not want.
Then, gins the straunger to record, the ring which he did see:
And fear doth make him think besids that ring the same to bee.
Which he did geve Jenevora, wherfore through every part:
Of his distemperd limmes, proceede an ake, and deadly smart.
From head, and hart, doth passe also a could, and lothsome sweat:
And temples both, and pulses two, refuse their lively heate.
His heare right up, his eyes do stare, his teeth he joyneth fast:
Much like a man distraught of wits, and holsome reason past.   [F4ᵛ]
Sometimes, (for lacke of breath) he lies berevd of lively sprightes:
And in his rage, lyke frantike man, his careful head he smyghtes.
And when his fittes be of least force, then with a panting hart:
Unto himselfe in secret wyse, these woords he doth impart.
Oh deepe disceit, oh hidden guile, oh falshood furie fell,
Oh cruell spight, condemned be thy ghost to lothsome hell:
That so canst fawn on simple wight with pleasant smilyng chere,
And with a hart invenemed, to kyll that houlds the deare.
Oh wretch, I scorne the present joy and eke thy Princely state:
And happy thrise wer these my eyes, to see thy latest fate.
Consumed be thy cherefull health, and sicknes seale thy corse:
Let sadnes, from eche part of thee, all pleasure quite devorse.
Converted be the cristall hewe, to foulest colour vyle:
And all diseases rule in thee, when health is in exile.
For thou (oh careles wretch) hast forst my limmes that lyvde in joy)
To taste the most unquiet rest, that any can anoye.   [F5ʳ]
And as he would have furder said, from stringes of swelled hart:
A deadly grone proceedes, and eke most scorning sobbes depart.
And therwithall, oh death (quoth he) wreake on my corse thy will,
Asunder sheare my vitall threed: oh Atrapos doo kill.
The most unhappiest creature, that treades on sinfull soyle:
And you oh sisters cut the thread, and ease me of this toyle.
Thus whilst he waies yᵉ brightnes of this goodly Diamond:
(Dispairing wise) infective feare doth nye his wittes confound.
But when he doth call unto mynde, what friendly actes have past,
Twixt him and his Jenevora, he calles his wittes at last.
To him, and then, his lavish tounge he ginnes for to reprove:
And saies, yᵗ nought but tride disceit, should faithfull friendes so move.
And then he gan to dought beside, if that same weare the ring:
That earst was his, which Polinesse from court with him did bring.

For though report, did blase (qd he) my gem to be the best:
Yet may an other be as good, though secretly it rest.   [F5ᵛ]
And dayly proufe, doth teach us eke, where Princes fansie frame:
There goes away the victory, and gayne of greatest name.
And though it were the ring it self, that I did late enjoye:
Yet till I know more perfect proufe, it shall me not annoy.
For how can such assured signes of lasting amitie:
Be joynd with crabbed craftines and with such subtiltie.
Did not her letter show to me, a lovers true intent?
Did not the passion of her mynde to faithfull lynes consent?
Did she not vow (with drowned eies) she lothed filthy guyle?
And did she not perswade me eke, to shunne such treason vyle?
Could this proceed from double mynd could heavenly shape invent:
Such termes of truth, & afterwards to such disceit consent?
Can she, that since her infancie, was traind in Princely court,
(Wher wisdoms lore, & prudence skil, is used for disport)
Beare in her hart such fayned truth, and use such subtill witte?
Or els upon well meaning wight, such spightfull hatred spitte?   [F6ʳ]
Can craftines finde harborow, within so goodly shape?
When nature servde so worthy corpse could truth from her escape?
Can double dealing lodge within so worthy creature?
Who for her passing comelynes gaines lasting lyfe tindure?
No, no, I doo abandon now my former fonde conceit,
And eke the sparkes of black dispaire I will extinguishe strayt:
For tyll those eyes doo plainely see, or els those eares doo heare,
Disdainful lookes, or scornful woords such fittes shall not me deare.
Tyll then, (though some presuming there be of fained love)
From chosen choyse, & harts desire, no passion shall me move.
By this, the blustring blast is blown that so amazd the mynde:
And Delus from Orient seas, doth breath a pleasant winde.
The darksome clouds are drowned now, that trobled earst the ayre:
And hope with beames of joyful light, turnes stormes, to wether fayre.
But sleape [(] that doth disdaine to see an other, to possesse
The place which he by right should keepe) doth seeke for to
      redresse.   [F6ᵛ]
This injurie, and calles foorthwith, his mates in his affayres,
That drowsy dreame, & slumber sad, and with his friendly prayers,
Doth crave his aide, with forced might, to yelde to him againe:
The place which he by right should have, which others now doo gayne.
Therwith ould Slumber gan imploy, with careful mynd his might:
To conquer Hope or els to dye, himselfe amidst the fight.
And with his Ingin he doth scale the fort but meanly mande:
And through the wall doth make a way, for to conduct his bande.
This seene, poore Hope, (as vanquisht man) not able to defende

Him from the whyrling dartes, that Sleepe about his eares doth sende :
Doth yelde himselfe condicionally, that next to Slumber, hee
Within his batterd castell, may be second in degree.
The conquerour doth graunt here to poore Hope is peakte away :
And now doth Dreame amidst the presse, his drowsie part well playe.
But Night that is the generall of all this sluggish crewe,
Gan from the fardest Orient coast, the mornyng playnly vewe.   [F7ʳ]
Then (least he should to long abide) he sends the Herault out :
(The Oule) yᵗ with her croked trump cries Retreat to the rout.
Wherby, the armie leaves the land, and flittes to Leathian seas :
Wher they abide till Night againe, shall yeld them former ease.
The cocke (Auroras messenger) sends foorth from stretched throte :
With flickring wings, & roused lym his cherefull mornings note.
Hope heers this sound, & then he [knows] his foe is fledde away :
Wherfore within his secret cave, no longer he can stay.
But to his former crased fort, with hastie foote he plies :
Wher entring in, Ariodant, doth lie before his eyes.
Who was one of his souldiers, when that sleape did geve the foyle,
And taken eke a prisoner, as he for Hope did toyle.
But, by good hap, no harme he had, save only in his head :
A littell scarre, of fond dispayre, that drousie Dreame had made.
Him, Hope doth comfort as he can, and with a lustie cheare :
No harme, (qd he) dismay thee not, discharge this filthy feare.   [F7ᵛ]
Herewith, the seely crased man doth leave his easie bed :
And hath concluded secreatly, (within his vexed head)
To leave the Duke, and to returne unto the court agayne :
Least by his still abiding there, the Duke mought seeke a meane
To searcke of him the truth herein, which, though he loth to showe :
Yet mought such words proceed unwares as therby harme mought grow.
Wherfore, when Duke of Albany had left his chambers rest :
Ariodant, (with bowed knee, gan of his grace request.
For to depart, his license, and his favour for to have :
And he, (thogh with unwilling mind) doth graunt that he doth crave.
Thus leaves the straunger Polinesse and he with speed, to court
Doth plie againe for to renewe, his fourmer joye and spourt.
Yet can he not (by any meanes) the sight of showed ring
Forget, though hope with pleasant wordes, good signes of joye doth
    bring.
By this, he is aryvde amongst the crewe of Courtiers stout :
That joye to see him safe retournde among that lusty rought.   [F8ʳ]
His brother eke Lurcanio, (inforst by course of kynde)
Doth welcome home Ariodant, with joyfull pleasant mynde :
And of such jestes as happened, since he did leave the court :
Unto his brothers lustinge eares, he makes along report.

But he, (this carefull lover) that is ny caught with dispayre,
Doth somon all his wittes at once, to helpe in this affayre.
And sith upon two fickell pointes, his present state dependes :
To take advise or he beginnes, his wyly head intendes.
I Nede not now for to recount, what guyle Duke Polynesse
Did use, with Princes Dyamond, tannoy his bidden gesse.
Nor how he faild of his intent, ne of the diverse talke,
That now from Polinessos lippes, and now from straungers walke.
But al you know (my Lords) how yᵗ Ariodant did feare,
That this was the selfe Dyamond, he gave his Ladie deare.
Which fere, so tost his troubled brain that as a man forlorne,
He shuns eche youthfull companie and life he had in scorne.   [F8ᵛ]
To ease these fittes, two only wayes this carefull lover spies :
Wherof, (as present state did crave) he gan this to devise.
Firstly, thinks he, if with my pen I causles should accuse :
Or els in presence, by complaint, I blameles should abuse.
The Princes grace, to whom I must accombt me chiefly bound :
Whose zelous mynd, (except I faile) I faithfull oft have found.
If that I shuld once move (I say) these doughtfull thoughts of myne :
Under her grace, by letters sent, or els before her eyne.
For to accuse her troth, unknowne, then let us see the ende :
Hereof, and to what passe, our taunting tale would tend.
At first, (as well she mought in dede) she should bestow on me,
[A] fond suspecting lovers name : and most untrue to be.
That at the sight of every toye would take occasion :
To blame her troth, and eke to live in vile suspicion.
Then after that, for to withdraw her love so evell employd :
And eke repent that such an one, so long hath it enjoyd.   [G1ʳ]
Which if these eies shuld once behold these hands with bloudie knife
Shuld take revenge upon my tongue by ridding of my lyfe.
And if she graunt : (as vile dispayre perswades me for to deeme)
I mean, that she doth love this Duke and evell of me esteeme.
If this she say, what then tell me, whats then our remedy?
In faith by corsies, bane, or cord, to die in misery.
Againe, if to my self I should, these secrets sole impart :
Lettes see if this may change our fits or els our cares convert.
This charge (qd he) to make the salve that cures the burning wound :
Tasswage the humors cold, that doth the patient nye confound.
As hard it is to ease the wight, with freting furious meat :
Whom fevers force continually, to pining bones doth eate.
So hard it is, that silence which augments my misery :
Shuld salve yᵗ sore which nothing els but talke can remedy :
For see, as belching poyson broyles, within the panting brest :
And scorching heat, converts yᵉ helth, to most unquiet rest.   [G1ᵛ]

So do the cares of vexed mynd, consume the crased hart :
Tyll by disclosing of his griefe, he findes to ease his smart.
But if (as this my case doth stand) bewraying bringeth death :
Tweare better thus to prove the end then for to wast my breath.
They say, that corsy ministred, unto them poysoned corse :
Will coole the fearse contagious heat and quench the burning force.
Why may not then the troubled mind by silent tongue annoy :
That health, which silence banisheth, and doth the hart enjoy.
For if my doubtes be false indeed and she doth love me still :
What then but silence can prevayle, and bridell lavish will.
And if she use for disport, and scornes my proferd love :
The knowledge of the troth therin, a desperate death doth move.
Wheras, if yet my love cannot within her hart prevayle :
Yet silence, truth, and tract of time, hereafter may avayle.
Wherfore as reason seemes tagree unto a secret hart :
So from these lips, those leud conceits I mynd shall not depart.   [G2ʳ]
But, as before the newes I hard, so now amidst the crewe :
Of courtly dames, my wonted sports I will forthwith renewe.
This last devise thus ended hath his argumentes eche one :
He listes no longer to consult, in hast he is forth gone.
The Princes court, wher no man is more welcomer then he :
As well unto Jenevora as to the Ladies free.
And ther, (like to his wonted guile) he dayly doth discourse :
Of histories : or riddels els he learnes to tel by course.
Thus leave I him that showes a face of perfect blisse and joye :
Though now & then amidst disportes dispayre doth him annoy.
And to the Duke I must agayne my solom verse returne :
That seeks (unhappy man) eche way, to cause the straunger mourne.
THough Polinesso wel had wayde, unto what small effect :
His former fond, and lewed devise, by yll luck was direct.
Though he perceivd how contrary eche point therof did prove :
And that no sight of gem, ne talke, could [ought] the straunger
    move.   [G2ᵛ]
Yet could he not slack lenger time, (inforst by jelousie)
But needs he must devise of newe, some other policie.
Wherfore, when that Ariodant was gone unto the court :
He leaves his home, and thether to, in hast he doth, resort :
Wher like unto his former wont, he feedes his doting eye
With Princes lookes, & takes therat a great felicitie.
And she agayn, (that knew right wel the skill of curtesie.)
Doth friendly intertaine the Duke into her company.
But furdest from her honest hart, (I dare avowe) was love :
To him whose graver yeeres, should shunne such youthfull toyes to move.
This aged amorous syre (I say) thus caught in Cupides net :

Cannot digest this jelousie, which he in straunger set.
But rather by the oft repayre, of yonge Ariodant:
New coals ar put to burning flames, that fire did not want.
Therfore when grief had long opprest this careful Duke his mynde:
In counsell to Ariodant, he thus doth spend his wynde.   [G3^r]
If that (quoth he) Ariodant, I thought my words would take,
More surer ground within thy mind then when I lastly spake
To thee, of this Jenevora, I would once more assay,
To turn thy youthful head from that that workes thy nown decay.
I see with sighes, & mark with mone (for so doth friendship move)
That nether talke, ne sight of ring can chaunge thee from this love.
I see, I see Ariodant, thou hast to good conceit,
And dost self wil to much imbrase that workes thine own disceit.
I see, how lightly thou regardst, that I tould late to thee:
I see thou scornst my sage advise and takst me false to be.
Els wouldst thou not so sodenlie forget that mought have taught
Thy skilles youth, to shun the bayte that hath thee captive caught.
But sith thus farre I have assaid to move thee to beleve:
That neither gifts, ne lookes, ne talk can ought thy Lady meve.
I will, (to quite my self of troth faith unfaind to thee)
Once more attempt a greter charge then thou before didst see.   [G3^v]
Thou knowst, at court within three dayes is kept a solom feast:
When eche to honour more to fame with bravest geare are drest.
Then will the Princes decked bee with Robes of shining gold:
And none so rich as she that day, ne goodlier to behold.
If then twixt nine, and ten at night, thou wilt repayre with mee:
Unto a secret place, when I a signe shall geve to thee.
Thy self shalt see Jenevora, and me Duke Polinesse
Imbrasing eche, and eithers corpse in others armes to presse.
So that at sight hereof thou wilt, geve place unto my love:
And leave these fickell fantasies that youthfulnesse doth move.
The Duke thus staies his filed tongue, and then Ariodant
This answere made unto his tale, that forst senses want.
Shew this (my Lord) & then (qd he) I yeld to your desire:
As one that is at your commaund, to what you list require.
Lo here my hand; (qd Polinesse) I sweare by this my Grace,
To show thee what I promised, at setted time and place: [G4^r]
But as to ease thee of thy griefe, I doo that reason nould:
So as thou art a gentilman, doo not my tale unfould.
The straunger graunts, & vows therto and thus they two depart:
Ariodant to chamber close, and Duke as likes his hart.
But when this thrise unhappy wight this carefull wretched man:
Was come unto his mourning den, he doth begin to scan.
Upon this false and forged tale, and despratly doth teare:

His trembling flesh, & rendes all that that he that day did weare.
His head he smites with bended fist, his feete he stampes on ground,
His holow sighes, & groning sobbes, from hart to skies resound.
Now groveling on the ground he crawles, and scrapeth with his nayles
The earth, and now againe him selfe his hasty hand assailes.
Now chokt w^t grief, he specheles lies as one berevd of breth :
And now to ende this furious fittes, he cries thus after death.
Oh death (quoth he) the ende of cares if ever thou didst graunt
Unto a wofull wretches will, that waylings doth not want.   [G4ᵛ]
If ever thou didst yelde unto, a haples mysers hest,
Or if unto the vexed corse, thou ever yeldest rest :
Graunt now to me (unhappiest slave) whose panges of pining payne,
Is more then natures kyndly course can brooke or els susteine :
A fatall push at last for all, and ende oh death this care,
Dispatch this lothsome lingryng life geve me this only share,
With fatal dart, (oh gentill death,) let lively bloud depart
By streames, out of this carcas vile and slyse this trembling hart.
Thou dolefull bel ring out at last, my last deperting knil :
Or lyving els close me in grave, my mouth with earth do fill.
But unto her, that causer is of this my mortall strife :
Oh death geve crooked aged limmes, with lothsome lingring lyfe.
For she it was, that straunged me from pleasant Italy :
And forst me like a banisht wight, to lyve in straunge countrie.
She, she, berevd from me my blisse, she brought to me this care,
She hath restraynd from me my joy, and caught me in the snare.   [G5ʳ]
Her smiling lookes, her frendly stile, and eke her vowed truth :
Hath brought me in this misery, alas the more my ruth.
Oh hart more hard than Adamant, oh false dissembling tongue,
Oh painted face, (whose worthinesse fame so far of hath Runge)
False [Creseids] gain, be thy reward, that art more false then she :
And worthier a thousand fold, a Leper for to be,
My carefull head cannot devise, lyke plagues for thy desert :
Ne yet my tongue declare the halfe, of thy deserved smart.
When first, these wretched eyes of myne did see that craftie corse :
And when this head did so beleve, thy lines of faithles force.
Would God this hand, had pearst this hart, with carving bloudie knife :
Or els that Lions tearing jawes had rid me of my life.
Oh haples wretch Ariodant that by the heavens consent,
Must work thyne own unhappines, through lothsome loves torment.
Oh abject slave, whose fortune is to fall into her hand :
That neither knows her self, ne yet a friend doth understand.   [G5ᵛ]
Thrise happy hadst thou ben, when that to love thou gavest thy mynde :
That nature had closd up thyne eares, and that thou hadst ben blinde.
But oh what gaynes this lavish talke? what profittes wish, and would :

When judge, upon condemned wight, hath dreadfull sentence tould?
Dispatch therfore, thou dastard slave, geve ende unto thy care:
Play morderer, with stabbing knife, the vaines a sunder share.
What, doest thou joye in miserie, that fearefull hand doth stay?
Or knowest thou any remedy, to vanquish death away?
Doth any hope remayne as yet to comfort thee with all?
Doth any sparke of blisse appeare, that may to thee befall?
Hast thou not hard thine own decay, and lacks ther ought but sight:
And canst thou live for to behould, that foule and filthy spight?
Thou doughst belike deceitfulnes, in Polinessos talke?
Who, as his willing hart did wish, thou thinkst his tongue did walke.
To ease thy heavy mynde therin content I am to stay:
But that once seene prepare thy self, for sight of Dismall day. [G6r]
And with a grisly grone he endes, his carefull heavy plaint:
And scorching sighes, & deadly sobbes do forse his members faint:
And overcome with griefe of mynd, his wery limmes have founde
A slumbring sleape, wherin he lies, as caught in mortall sound.
Thus leave I this Ariodant, upon his carefull bed:
Amidst a heape of dreadful dreames, that swarme in vexed head.
And once agayne unto this Duke, (this false perjured man)
I must returne to blase againe, his treason as I canne.
Therfore when false dissemblyng Duke, had easd his swelled minde:
By belching out these carefull newes, and vouched othes, to blynde
The more, this true dispairyng wight: he byddes him then adewe,
And trackes no tyme, ne lettes aught slippe, his purpose to pursue.
Wherfore the even before the feast, Dalinda he ought spies:
And thus amidst his other talke, this tale he gan devise.
As joyfull newes as ever came to thee Dalinda earst,
Or gladder farre then ever yet, thy listing eares have pearst. [G6v]
I will import to thee [(] my nowne and chiefest faithfull friend)
With whome, the rest of this my lyfe, in wedlocke I will spend.
Leave of therfore, those musing dumps, that trouble so thy minde:
And to my happy tale se that, thy open eares be inclinde.
Thou long hast seene with griefe (I know) what signes of love have past,
Betwixt thy Ladies mistres, and twixt me thy friend (at last,)
Thou knowst, how long I suid, and servd, her grace for to obteyne:
And eke thou knowst how loyall I, all that time did remayne,
Thou knowst (myne own) that only was, the chiefest cause that I
So slenderly requited thee, and thy great curtesie.
But see, as fonde affections forse, and signes of seemly grace,
As bewties beames, assotted me, to serve that froward face:
So now (at last) that coyeishnes, and her disdainfull mynde,
Hath turnd my hart intrapped long, that bewtie so dyd blynde
To lothsomnes, and lyke disdayne, and now I am as free,

(Thank God) as when indiffrent eye did egally eche see. [G7ʳ]
Wherfore, in signe of this dispite, and of more careles hart:
What in my mynde I have devisd, to thee I will impart.
Thou knowst (qd he) ther is in court a row of houses ould:
That wast do lie, unoccupide, unable scarse to hould.
Them selves a loft upon the ground a place of no repayre:
Except with dogges, or vermyn vyle or els with fowles of thayre.
Against these rotten walles ther is, (as thou right well dost know)
Imbossed ought from joyned frame, a stately bay window.
Which is as voyd as is the rest, a lodging fit for none:
At that self place, I have devisde that thou thy self alone:
About the houre of ten at night shall mete thy Polinesse:
Tomorow, dekt with princes roabes and eke thy self shalt dresse.
With glistring cals and juels rich, with those she ware that day:
Wher I in scorne of Princes will with thee Dalinda play.
And eke imbrase thy worthy corpse, as deare to me as lyfe:
Of whom (as sone as time shal serve) I mynde to make my wife. [G7ᵛ]
This is theffect of my devise, this is the summe and all:
Of that which bringeth libertie, to thee that now art thrall.
For here in court thou subject art, to beck and to obey:
Wher next to me in Albany thou chief shal beare the sway.
Therfore if sparke of faithfulnes lodge in thy gentell brest:
If ever yet to pleasure me, thy friendship hath ben prest.
Fayle not with corded ladder and with Princes brave attire,
At that same place and at that time, to yeld to my desire.
Said crafty Duke, & therwith staies, his false deceitfull tongue:
The sting wherof, so fervenly hath our Dalinda stung.
And eke that vile ambition, hath so infect the mayde:
That presently she yeldeth to, all that before he sayd.
Thus hath the Duke, (as hart would wish) performd his enterpryse:
And finisht hath his false request as he could best devise:
And now unto his careles couch with easd mind he hies:
And lieth til the golden globe, doth drive night from his eyes. [G8ʳ]
The irksome shade, that so annoyes the heavy pensive wight,
Forsakes the skies, & morning now hath banisht drousy night.
The joyfull daye doth show his face, the gromes no lenger lye,
But to performe his charge, ech one with carefull mynde doth plie.
The massie roabes for princes grace from wardrobe are out brought:
The borders brave of gouldsmithes craft, with stone and pearle
    [ywrought:]
The Jueler delivers to the Ladies of the court,
With tablet, cheine, & braslettes dekt, with stones of diverse sorte.
With those the careful ladies dresse, Jenevora that day,
That rather seemes of heavenly mould, then of dame natures clay.

Thus drest, this peereles princes plies for to perfourme hir rights,
To chapel, well accompanied with rought of Scottish knights.
There all the morning she doth spend as temples hestes require,
And prayers sayde, to court againe the Princes doth retire.
But what needes longer stay herein, what booteth to report.
The dayntie cates, servd in that day, and of the diverse sort.   [G8ᵛ]
As well of pleasant Bacchus cups, as Ceres dainty dish:
And of the dulcet musickes skill as sweet as eare would wish.
Sith far from blis my stile is changd this day hath causd that care:
That neither head can well devise ne pen can well declare.
Therfore let courtiers joy in court and geve me leave a while,
To write of hopeles wretches haps, whom treason did beguile.
The setted time by Polinesse approcheth on a pace:
When straunger shuld behold yᵉ Duke the Princes to imbrace.
Wherfore as one not well assurd of Scottish faithfulnes:
Ne certain that the Duke did meane as late he did expresse.
Least that (I say) in some dark place he had imbusht a crewe:
Of traytors to invyron him, when he this sight should vewe.
He comes unto his brother then, whose might he knew right well,
Would succour him assuredly, if any then would mell.
Whose company he craves that night when he should see him go:
With Polinesse, and that he would bring swoord with him also. [H1ʳ]
Lurcanio, whose lyfe and death, his brother mought commaund
With willing mynd consents unto Ariodants, demaund.
Duke Polinesse, not careles of thappointed houre and time:
(Which now is come) when yᵗ [he] shuld performe his filthy cryme.
Comes to this most unhappy man, and biddes him folow fast:
If that he list to see the thing, wherof he tould him last.
Ariodant that long had stayd to see the carefull ende:
Obeys the Duke, and after them Lurcanio doth wend.
To desert houses they are come the Duke hath brought his mate
Unto a place direct against the window which of late
I tould you of, wher (Princes lyke) Dalinda should appeare:
Before yᵉ Duke, dect with those robes their Prince that day did weare.
Ariodant thus plaste, the Duke doth bid him cast his eye
Upon that window, wher (quoth he) thou shalt thy Lady spy.
Lurcanio that longs to see the sequell of this jest:
Is come within ten feete wheras Ariodant doth rest.   [H1ᵛ]
Wher he unseene may vew likewise that window at his will:
Ther secretly the straunger standes, that doughtes some present ill.
Duke Polinesse, no sooner leaves the pencive lovers place:
But to thappointed window, he directes his feete apase.
Wher he had not remayned long, but see, with glistring light
Of gould, Dalinda doth appeare lyke angell to the sight.

And as the Duke had geven in charge so she in bravest wyse:
With shining robes, w^t Diamonds set that gleme before the eyes
Lyke burning torch in winter night is come into this place:
Wher Polinesse like Judas doth her scorned limmes imbrace.
And to the end, the straunger should more perfectly behould:
His loving toyes, her kisses eke. and how his armes do fould
Her griped wast he doth approch as nere as windowe will
Geve leave to him, to straungers sight that he mought vew his fill
Therof, & how she claspes her armes about his stretched necke:
Whose store of kisses do declare, her mynd voyd of suspect.   [H2^r]
Lurcanio, whose glasing eyes are not unoccupied:
Upon the window staring stands wher he hath now espied
Jenevora, (as he did deeme) because of Juels bright:
And eke the golden roabes did shine so lively in his sight.
But for to know, who so did tosse the Princes rich attyre:
His staring eyes and greedy lookes by no meanes could aspire.
This sight, thus seene, Lurcanio (accompting brothers health
As life, to him,) in secret wise (unknown) is come by stealth.
Wher most unhappy lover stayes, who seing all this jest:
As man distraught, his rapiere he in hastie hand hath prest.
And scorning lenger life, hath set the hilts upon the ground:
In minde by falling on the point to carve his fatall wound.
And as he did on groning blade his desperate body bend:
(Behold the mercie great of God) his brother doth defend.
His trembling hart from deadly pushe, by holding in his armes
His falling brest, and that once done he thus his brothers charmes. [H2^v]
What devlish act annoieth thus thy head berevd of witte:
What desperate joy hath taunted thee what foule and lothsome fitte
Hath so beguile thy sences al, that thus (unhappy wight)
Thou sekst by this untimely death thy passions vile to quite.
[Is] this the ende of all our toyle? is this our travels gayne?
Is lothsome death thy just desert and is an endles payne
A gwardon fit for me, (thinkst thou) that leaving native soyle:
(Like banish slave) shal live in court, consumd with cares tourmoyle
For losse of thee, whom as my life, thou knowst I hould as deare?
And shall I live to see the day, the heavie newes to beare
Unto our carefull pensive friendes, that by his own consent:
Their wretched friend Ariodant, his latest dayes hath spent?
Or reckles friend of brothers life, and could thy hart agree:
To leave thy brother destitute, of friend in straunge countree?
Or if thou hadst no whit esteemd thy faithfull brothers life:
Could Ladies falshod force thee run, on point of persing knife?   [H3^r]
What [lure] hath inchanted (tell) thy skill in wisedomes lore:
What madnes hath intoxicate thy pleasant thoughtes so sore.

That neither losse or joyfull lyfe no feare of dampned ghost :
Can change my mynd from this intent (oh wretch of wretches most)
Can bewtie bleare thy wilfull eye and [force] thee for to love :
And cannot sight of foule deceit, from amours force thee move.
Can fansie frame that amietie by sight of seemely grace :
Which present guile, and filthy fact, by no meanes can displace?
And canst thou wreake such sharpe revenge upon thy giltles hart :
And see her love that is the ground of this thy present smart?
Roote out (I say) such ugly thoughtes from bounds [of] troubled minde :
And seke by reasons sweete advise some holsome salve to finde.
If eye did chuse a faithfull friend and fansie did agree :
If hope intiste thy drowned hart, to serve assuredly.
Let now to suer signes of hate, let proufe of lyke disdayne :
Lodge scornefulnes in careles hart for love long vowde in vayne.   [H3ᵛ]
So shalt thou dryve these dreadfull panges, out from thy panting brest :
And to thyne owne Lurcanio, bring lasting joy and rest.
Sayd carefull soule Lurcanio, unto Ariodant :
That hath as many eares to heare, as hath the Adamant.
So altred hath this sight his wittes and eke his stayd intent :
That sage advise was bootles geven, the sequell to prevent.
Yet lest his brother mought perceive his changeles will to die :
And least by striving with his force, he mought his purpose spie.
Thogh overcome with mortal pangs he mute and dombe doth stand :
(In signe of grace, he puts his blade into his brothers hand.
That don, from that unhappy place to chamber close they hie :
And (as the time of night did crave) to bed they both do plie.
Lurcanio (in hope his wordes had changd his brothers mynd)
(Nought doughting of the present il) a quiet sleape doth finde.
But he, surprisd in dreadful thoughts with visage pale and wanne
In stead of sleape, in frantike mind a thousand tymes doth banne. [H4ʳ]
The day which first gave light to him he curseth eke the teate
That in his fansie did geve, to him his sucking meate.
As oft he bannes his damned eyes, that so could fix their sight :
And eke his tongue yᵗ sude for grace, of one so false a wight.
He curseth now his open eare that so did marke her guyle :
And hastie hart that trusted so her lippes so fraught with wile.
What shuld I say, both head, & hand, and all he could invent :
In steed of blisse, and wishes good, he doth with curse torment
So in this wise eche night is spent and day renues agayne :
His wonted course, but night, ne day, can chaunge this lovers paine,
But still upon some present death, he gladly doth devise :
As one that only findes that salve, to ease his scorching cries.
Wherfore to drive suspition the more from brothers brest :
He cloaks his care, and riseth when, Lurcanio leaves his rest.

And finding then occasion to leave his companie:
He hies in hast by wilfull death to ende his miserie.   [H4ᵛ]
As stroken hart, whose bleading wound, declares a present death,
With reckles feete climmes hill and vale, whilst he hath life and breath:
As greadie Beare, that is berevd, (whilest she doth raunge for pray)
Of littell whelp, doth howle & roare, and dreadfully doth bray:
As Turtel Dove that is beguild of hoped faithfull mate,
In pining wyse misliking spendes, hir tyme tyll latest fate:
So fares it with Ariodant, this wretch full fraught with woe,
Whose trembling feete no soner had left poore Lurcanio:
But out unknown to fields he hies, and raunging here and there,
Like frantike man, now runs he fast and now (as caught with feare)
He creeping by yᵉ ground doth crawl and now (like one agast)
He staring stands not moving joynt and now he hies as fast.
But styl upon this tragedy, upon his [setted] part,
His heavie mynde, is occupide, and eke his desperat hart.
Wherfore, at last approching neare unto a River deepe:
He doth conclude his last devise, no lenger now to sleepe.   [H5ʳ]
But calling to a traveler that then past by the waye:
With broken sighes and faltring tongue he thus to him doth say.
My friend (qd he) although unknown perhaps I am to thee,
Yet let me crave thy curtesie, thus much to doo for me:
That is, that thou forthwith wilt go, unto the Scottish court,
Wher from me, to Jenevora, thus much thou shalt report.
Through to much sight Ariodant, hath founde untimely death:
And yelded to the greadie streame, his last departing breath,
This same is all, this doo [performe], let pitie move thy mynde:
Sith power wants for to requite, that friendships lore doth bynde.
This said, the cloudie sighes proceede from scorched hart by heapes:
And therwithal deepe sobs & grones, from gasping throte out leapes.
The traveler, agast to heare, these straunge and careful newes,
Doth feele his vitall senses fayle and falles in mortall mewse.
And coming to him selfe againe in faire and friendly wise,
(Lyke to his skill) he uttereth what harme therof might rise.   [H5ᵛ]
As first, his death once bruted foorth, his lyfe is had in scorne,
And ther with lasting memorie, with liveles limmes is worne
Except report reprochfull blast in every coast doth sound:
How wilfully Ariodant, his desperate course hath dround.
Besides the daunger of the soule, he puts into his mynde:
And eke the terrour of the payne, that is therfore assingde.
But care of heaven, or dought of hel, is fardest from his thought:
And how yᵉ world wold deeme of him he neither careth ought.
Wherfore when no perswasion could chaunge his black intent:
With drowned eyes, yᵉ straunger doth to his request consent.

Then from the toppe of craggy rock, he lookes to streame belowe :
& stretching [foorth] his shaking armes, him selfe foorthwith doth throwe
Amidst the streame, y^t foulds his corse and ther withall doth sinke
Unto the ground, & ther remaynes, which causd the straunger think
That gredi goulf had chokt his breth and that he had ben dead :
Wherfore he hies unto the court, with minde complet with dread.   [H6^r]
Ariodant, (though noble hart, did scorne for to remayne
In such distres, and rather chusd by death to ease his payne,)
Yet feeling pangs of lothsome death, which kinde could not indure :
He strives againe to get that life, which care did earst procure
To banish from his vexed limmes, and using lothed might :
By force of armes & stretched legges lyfe ther hath won the fight.
And death is fled, with whom retires that foule and dreadfull thought :
Which carefull wretch Ariodant to deare well nie had bought.
Thus quite from death, the straunger now doth sommon wits againe,
To counsell what is best to doo amidst these stormes of raine.
First, pleasure biddes him to repaire againe to lusty court,
Wher sone thou shalt distroy (qd he) these thoughts through pleasant
    sport.
And sith thou art by skill instruct, to shunne false Venus bayte :
Perswade thy selfe, the blynded boy no more for thee will wayte.
With that conceit affection, doth seeme for to agree,
Although in reasons they be all, and therfore thus saith hee.   [H6^v]
Now knowest thou Lurcanio wil brooke these heavy newes,
What griefe of minde shal he indure what torments will he use
(Thinkst thou) [( ] when he shal heare thy death) to ryd his lothed life?
The best is thinke by pining dayes, if not by persing knife.
And I (qd vertue) can not yeld, unto your joynt consents :
I see small reason to induse me, to so straunge intents.
We say, that man thryse happy is whome others proved harme,
From fallyng hedlong to such haps, can warne and warely charme.
The court was causer of thy care, by court did spryng thy paine :
Then let these daungers of the court from court straunge the againe.
The wyly byrd can shunne the net which earst enthrald her so :
The sely mouse once caught in trap, can shunne the guyle also.
But vessels sayd with sower wyne, kepe still their former tast :
And that which in the boane is bred, from thence is hardly plast.
So hard it is to maister love which rooted is in hart :
But rather by continual sight is growen a greater smart.   [H7^r]
And as unto Lurcanio, how he these newes will take :
I dought it not but for thy death he great complaint wil make.
But for to say, in desperat wise, he will him selfe confound,
Thats very straunge, & hard to make that in myne eares to sound,
He loves thee as a brother ought, (so nature doth him move)

But selfe love toucheth nearer kinde this tale thou true shalt prove.
At first thy death is griefe to him, els kindly force is gone:
But as the wearing time doth waste so doth abbridge his mone.
Wherfore leave lusty blouds in court let brother morne his fill:
Let fading worldly pleasures be, and herke than to my skill:
Learn thou w^t remnant of thy daies, the blissed sacred lore,
Seke now at last tappease the hevens whom thou offendst so sore.
So shalt thou learne by lyfe to die, and die to lyve in joy:
So shal not then thy fleshly lustes, thy sinfull ghost annoy.
This sentence was no sooner tould but for to show consent,
Eche lymme and joynt are eased wel and lyppes pronounce, con-
    tent,

[H7^v]

The Parlament thus ended is, to vertue stranger yeldes:
And running here and there abrode amidst the desert fields:
He doth at last a sheapard spie, whome he in friendly wyse
Salutes, and after that, he craves the sheapard to advise
Him of some holy place, wheras a man mought leade his lyfe
In quietnes, and wher he mought abandon worldly strife.
Upon this hill (qd shepard then) if that thou list to go:
Thou shalt ther find an Hermetage an aged man also,
That there alone doth passe away his wery aged tyme.
In prayers much devoutly for remisse of former cryme.
This known, Ariodant doth leave, the Sheapehard with farewell
And mountes on hauty hyll, wheras the Hermite poore doth dwell.
And finding him amidst his beades with hartie greatings made:
The goodly courtier strayns his spech and thus to him he sayde.
That god that form'd the erth & seas and framed man of nought.
Increase thy faith, and send thee that which thou so long hast
    sought

[H8^r]

Good father, though, (through tender age,) the frayle unbridled youth
Doth lacke the deepe discretion, to scanne and judge the truth:
And [though] the motions of the flesh provoke the fickle brayne
To light esteeme the heavenly foode, and honour fancies vayne:
Yet (you doo know) by turning oft, the true discourses ould
Of auncient actes, how God above, disdaynd not to unfoulde
His hidden secret mysteries unto the tender age:
When contrarie, he doth dispyse to shew that to the sage.
For proufe we neede none other shew then Daniell the childe:
Who savd Susanna from the flames and justice eke did [yelde],
Unto the aged Judges two, who fayling their intent:
Concluded to condemne to fyre the sily innocent.
So David, (in his infancie,) inspird with heavenly might:
Did conquer stout Goliaghs limmes in open combat fight.
Which prove not time, but godli gifts sent from the spring of grace:

Doo rule within the vertuous, and in his hart take place.   [H8ᵛ]
That hevenly beck, & fountain cleare hath moysted so my lust:
Oh father, that the vanities, (which late my ghost did rust,)
Are washt clean from my fretted hart, and now I am in mynd:
(If thou wilt graunt) by more advise more store of grace to finde.
And sith the chast and secret lyfe, abandons fading wealth:
And poore and sparing abstinence lettes in the lasting health:
Deny me not thy felowship, graunt me thy company:
Helpe now to save a sinfull soule that craves a remedy.
So shall I bridell foule desire, and thou do service great
To him, that hath prepard for us (I hope) a heavenly seat.
He said, and staid, and Hermit then with bended lookes to skies,
With heaved armes, & watrie plants directs his tale this wyse.
That faith, which Samuell possest, God graunt thee to enjoy:
God send thee Samsons strength to help when feend would thee annoy.
As wise as Salomon the wise, as chast as Jacobs sonne:
As constant as Abednago: whom, fyrie flames did shunne.   [I1ʳ]
Hould here my shaking hand (qd he) I do imbrace thy will:
Be thou to me a lasting mate, if deeds thy words fulfill.
Thus is our lusty courtier made, (by taking small degree)
An hermit, poore, and learneth now a holy man to be.
Whom I must leave amidst his rootes (in steede of dainty cates)
And now unto the traveler, (that is come to the gates.
Of Scottish court) I must retourne, who craves in gentill wise
To speake with fayre Jenevora that careles doth devise.
Of sundry sports amongst her mayds she is advertised
Of traveler, and sends for him he comes nye chockt with dred.
And after humble dutie done, and trembling every vayne:
With hollow voyce, his paly lippes he thus to speake did strayne.
What newes (oh Princesse) I do bring what message I declare:
If good, or bad, as tis unknown, so let thy highnes spare.
The skilles messenger, that is by faithfull promise bound:
This ruthful message to pronounce, and in thine eares to sound,   [I1ᵛ]
The same, which wretched cative I, with these myne eyes did see:
Which as they are, and as I was commaunded, take from mee.
Through to much sight, Ariodant hath found untimely death:
And yelded to the greedy streame his last departing breath:
This he did say, which I have showd unto your majestie:
And then he lept into the streame, and died, (oh ruth to see)
Now to your skilfull judgements, I oh Ladies do commit:
To show upon these carefull newes what kinde of cruell fit.
Opprest unhappy Princes ghost, what thoughts of endles payne,
What scorching grief, what frosen feare within her temples rayne.
What flashing blud doth boyle within her limmes of heavenly mould:

What trembling dread doth shake eche joynt then nipping ise more could.
Such tearmes (I say) of mynde opprest I leave unto thy skill:
Oh Phenix byrd, that of like joyes for friend hast found thy fill.
But sith (my Lordes) your doughtfull heades can hardly deeme such
    fittes:
To dwell in Ladies pleasant heades, I will inforce my wittes.   [I2ʳ]
To tell you here the whole discourse of her lamenting case:
And eke what pensive passions love within her hart did place.
This message dark, pronounced thus, the messenger departs:
But message he doth leave behinde: to sauce the Princes smartes.
The sound wherof no soner had perst through her listing eare:
But after it into her head do folow stormes of feare.
Which makes the golden frisled heare right up in head to stand:
And fury forst her christall eyes, to burne like fire brand.
Out from her nose & mouth doth pas, a streame of gushing bloud:
And eke like rubie trickling droppes from bathed eyes do scud.
From gasping throate no breath proceedes, eche limme hath lost his life:
Twixt sobbing hart and dreadfull death, appeares a mortall strife.
Her feble joynte, with senceles corse, doo founder to the ground:
In fine, eche peece, eche part, and all are fallen into a sound.
But (Lord) what sturre the Ladies keepe what mones the maydes do
    make:
What skreekes, and cries, they send to skies, what carefull paynes they
    take,   [I2ᵛ]
For to releave their mistres deare, whom they did love so well:
Doth passe my wit, and skilles head, in writing plaine to tell.
For one with careles hand her tender fingers wring:
And she with pinching of her nose doth make the bloud out spring.
This matron bends her heavy head, down to her crased brest:
And this, her joyned jawes and teeth, doth force with key to wrest.
She cales for Aqua fortis, and Jenevora she cryes:
And she in steed of helping hand, spends teares from drowned eyes
For troth no old experimen that dying fittes could cure:
No teares, no cries, no dolefull tune, that sorow can procure:
But these bewayling Ladies, have at full attempted, and
With willing hart & carefull mynd, assayd and tane in hand.
Through which attempts, & using so her sensles figure fayre:
Out from her chafed mouth doth pas a slender breathing ayre.
And then her setted eyes in head, she heavily doth roule:
As thogh she presently would yelde unto the heavens her soule.   [I3ʳ]
And thus with groning voyce she sayes, oh haples harmefull handes:
That would not suffer death to rid my ghost from carefull bands.
Oh careles foes what profittes you, to see me diyng live:
What shal you gaine to see this hand my deadfull stroake to give.

Oh dismall day of my distresse, oh my Ariodant:
Nought els but my departing soule, thy flying ghost doth want.
Which, (sith thy life was my increase) thy death shall now inforce:
By bloudy hands to yeld to thee, with wounding of my corse.
But oh, what sight so much annoyd thy comely personage:
That unto thy Jenevora, thou couldst doo such outrage?
In drowning y^t which I more deere then friends or life did hould,
The sight wherof broght helth to me, when I did it behould.
What sight so vile, the vew wherof could maister so thy mynde,
That unto me thy vowed friend thou couldst be so unkinde?
Did ever signe of foule untruth, appeare before thy sight?
Did ever deed or word make false that faith that I did plight?   [I3^v]
To thee: and which I never sought since first I bound to lose?
Dorst ever yet these lippes of myne, presume for to disclose.
(Till now to late) our secret love? [(] oh speake thou flying sprite,
And ease me of this one conceit, as thou art faithfull knight)
To late, to late. (a lasse) I crie, in vayne I wast my breath:
But out to soone: to soone, (a lasse) I wayle thy cruell death.
And shall I live berevd of friend, shall mourning let in age?
And ist enough with heavy mones, my passions to asswage?
No, no, myne owne Ariodant my first approved frend:
And eke the last with whom I mynd my dayes in love to spend:
Even as thy lively feature, inforst me to thy love:
So shall thy death, let in my death, as time right well shall prove.
And as she did begin at first, nie chockt with mortall sound:
Even so she endes her heavy plaint, with falling down to ground.
Amidst [these] stormes of deadly grief and passions stoarde with payne:
Report with treble sounding voyce his yelling throate doth
    strayne.   [I4^r]
And puttes into eche open eare, how that by self consent:
Amidst the streame Ariodant, his latest dayes hath spent.
And now into Lurcanios eares, this heavy newes he blowes:
And how, & when, he drownd him self to him he plainly showes.
Wherwith ye carefull brother caught, with sting of pearsing death:
Resines his warlike force, and falles therwith downe to the earth.
Wher after many griping grones, inforst by grief of mynd:
His noble hart hath wonne by force his banisht breathing wynd.
But festred lies in hart the care, that troubles every vayne:
And deep in thought is lodgd ye cause, of this newe proved payne.
The force wherof so calmed hath his fierce coragious hart:
That see from eyes long time dryd up, a floud of teares depart.
Which mixed are with heavy sobbes from manlike broyling brest:
And compast in with smoking sighes, and flames of great unrest.
All these in dungeon deepe below Alecto fiers espies:

Whose nature is, in vexed hart pale hatred to devise.   [I4ᵛ]
Wherfore (hir snaky heares wound up) she leaves hir lothsome denne
And flies unto the Scottish court: wheras, Lurcanio then
Was heavely bewayling of his wretched brothers death,
To whome (like aged matron dight,) she spends this divelish breath.
When shall thy childish plaints have ende? when shal thy cares be spent?
When shal thy latest sighes be brethed that tende to smal intent?
Oh, false unto thy brothers ghost, doo womens mones suffise,
To answer that, which for revenge to thee eche houre cries?
Shal murder thus be suffered? shall bloudie hands enjoye
A longer life, is this the love thou sekst for to imploye
On him, that (whilst he lived on erth) held thee then lyfe more deare?
Is this a brothers just rewarde? dost thou such friendship beare
Unto thy most abused friend? and canst thou live to see
Thy brother dead, his foe alyve? hym stervd, and she stylle free?
Hath nature formd thee void of witte? (oh cruell to thy kinde)
Hath pitie so assotted, this thy worthy warlike minde?   [I5ʳ]
That neither brothers amitie, ne lynke of justice lore,
Can move thee for this foule offence just judgement to implore?
Leave thou these lamentations long, drie up these childish teares,
And spedely see that thou put into thy sovereignes eares:
How that the Prince Jenevora dishonored hath her state:
In feeding her dishonest lust with one thou sawest of late,
And that of body she is false, see thou defend with force:
So shalt thou yelde a just rewarde, by burning of her corse.
This spightfull spight, thus vomited from ugly lothsome pate
A snake she pulles which for to move Lurcanio more to hate.
She throwes into his bosome right, wher stinging it remaynes:
And poysneth so eche joynt & limme, and swelles so all his vaynes,
That raging, (like a frantike beast,) unto the king he hies:
To whome, his dutie finished, this tale he doth devise.
That fayth (oh king) which subjectes bare unto their soveraigne:
That love that to their Princely state, within their harts remayne. [I5ᵛ]
That care which to their high renowne, and honor eke they have:
And last, that great regard they use, their vertue still to save:
Hath forst my trembling tongue to speake against the lust of mynde,
And charged my closed lippes to tell, that duties force doth binde.
Which newes, though some unrest do bringe unto your horie heares,
Yet yelding justice for the same, gaynes life that never weares
Oh worthy king, and my liege Lord (though but alyde by vowe)
The noble intertainment, which I have received of you,
Commaundes me not to hide a fact, so heinous from your grace,
Though deede be done by such anone, as comes of royall race.
Whordom (oh king) committed by the Prince Jenevora

It is, that so hath moved my tongue and lippes from longer staie.
Which these my eyes (to soone) have seene at place and time unfit :
In proufe wherof, loo here my gage, I will my lyfe commit
Into his hands, that gives the palme unto the faithful wight,
And yeldes the gayne of victorie to him that fights in right.   [16ʳ]
I neede not now declare what thoughtes oppresse the pensive king,
Ne what ill rest to aged head, these careful newes doo bring :
Sith prone it is to testie age to take in fretting wise
A small offence, and every fault is great before their eies.
Wherfore his present panges I passe, I leave his heavy hart
Wrapt in with web of carefulnes, and gript in grave of smart :
And to this kings reply, I will direct my penne againe,
Who pausing long from carefull thoughts at last he doth refraine,
                                            and thus he sayes.
LUrcanio, thy service good and faithfull unto me,
Doth argue in my doughtfull head, thy minde from falshood free :
But if my age be not disceivd, if fame doo not beguile
My hoping hart, such shameful actes are fardest in exile
From hir whom thou hast now accusd whose parents goodly age,
Was never justly taynted with a deede of such outrage.
Wherfore sith doughtfull yet it lies, within our princely minde
And sith none but Lurcanio, this foule abuse doth finde   [16ᵛ]
We will before our sentence geven examine this accusd :
That hath by whordom (as thou saist) our state so much abusd.
And least thou deeme mee partiall, I do accept thy gage
Condicionly, that thou thy self, this proferd fight shalt wage
Against who listeth to mainteine her truth against thy might
(Like to our auncient laws ordeind) by force of combat fight.
And if thou gaine the victory, then she to flames of fire :
If vanquist thou, she free shall live, thou death shalt have for hire.
Which fight we wil shalbe performd upon the fifteenth day :
Ensuing next, when God (I trust) the right with right will pay.
So sayd, Lurcanio leaves the King, and to his chamber hies :
Wher for his brothers death he doth renewe his wonted cries.
But careful king, (when straunger was departed from his sight :)
(In minde to trie his truth herein) doth send a faithfull knight.
For carefull Jenevora whom messenger doth finde :
Amidst her maydes lamenting still with head to brest inclinde,   [17ʳ]
To whome his dutie finished, his message he doth show,
Theffect wherof Jenevora when perfectly doth knowe,
She wiping cleane her bathed chekes and trimmeth up her heare,
Doth so repaire unto the king, though with unchaunged cheare.
To whome, she is no sooner come, but voydance then is made
Of eche estate, and then the king with trickling teares thus sayde.

They say, that childe thrise cursed is, whose vile and vicious life,
Doth cause the loving parents dye consumde with carefull strife
Which endles grief, god grant (qd he) thy actes force me not prove,
But that thy hoped vertues doo, from such conceits me move.
Tis so (qd he) Jenevora whylst in our Princely court
We weard away our crooked age, lyke to our wonted sort :
Before our pretence doth appeare, the stout Lurcanio,
Who of free will dyd justifie and threw downe gage also
To prove : that thou hast don the deede that hath deserved fyre,
I meane that thou hast purchast deth through whordoms foule
    desire. [17ᵛ]
Which deede, him selfe did see he vowd at place and time unmeete
And judgement he did crave also for such offence most fitte.
Which judgement I have stayed yet, to heare what thou canst saye :
Why dreadful doome of present death, should longer for thee staye.
This sayd, the king complete with care doth staye his choked breath :
And feeles the force of mortall ache, and latest pangs of death.
But she, whose wretched ghost hath felt the worst of all her smart,
With countnance fearse (disdayning lyfe) all feare doth set appart,
And answers thus unto the king, my Lord and soveraigne.
Of catives all she wretch is most she feeles most store of payne.
Whose heavy hap doth rather bidde the tongue for to confesse
Untroth, then by accusing tale to pleade for her redresse,
Oh king, of whom this earthly shape by dome I doo enjoye,
Let not these latest woords of mine, thy Princely mynde annoy :
But heare indifferently what cares, thy childe doth now susteyne :
That rather seekes to suffer death, then long to taste this payne. [18ʳ]
My dread, and soveraine Lord and kyng thy skilfull horie heares
Know, well, how from the cradell up unto the latest yeares :
We subject are to every sinne, and thrald of natures kinde,
By thought, by woord, by deede, and sight unto the fancies blynde
Of worldly cares, and nought there is within our sinfull hart
But fancies fond, which reason willes should tast a lasting smart.
Such thoughts, such words, such deedes, and sights oh king have rulde
    in me :
And doo, and will, tyll of the yoke of life my limmes be free.
Amongst which sinfull passions, one most annoyed my minde,
One act ther is wherin (oh king) I greatest griefe doo finde :
Which sith both time & present state byds tell unto your grace,
I will disclose, & from my hart all damps of feare displace.
Wherby I shal drive dought (I trust) out from your doughtfull breast,
And make you privie of such haps as in me lurking reast.
Amongst the train of this your court and of your courtiers stout,
Amongst the worthy company of all the courtly rought : [18ᵛ]

There was (your highnes knowes right wel) one knight Ariodant:
In whom that should adorne a man, no gift at all did want.
A seemely wight, of spotles faith, although an alien borne:
Whose shape with thousand comely giftes dame nature did adorne.
His noblenes, his grace, and shape, enforce my virgins hart:
Long time to plunge in goulfs of care and tast of lovers smart.
He turnd my chast disposed mynde from thoughtes of maydens life:
And taught me seke to salve ye wound of Cupides fatall knife.
But see (the hevens I think it would) that stroke which pearst my brest,
Did carve in him a griesly gashe and in his hart did rest.
Thimpoisned push, which forced him to feele lyke fittes and payne:
And in like storms of troubled mind long time for to remayne.
Till y^t a means he found, which way he mought disclose his love
To me, and eke for to bewray, that Cupides force did move.
Which when I understood, no wight did ever tast like joye
As I (glad soule) that banisht then that earst did me annoy.   [K1^r]
And waying long his vertues great, and eke his good intent:
(Which caused my affection) at last I did consent.
Unto his love and choosing then him as my dearest frend,
I did conclude in wedlockes band, with him my life to spend:
But see the fruites of this our blisse, see here unstable state:
See, see (oh King) the end of all, this our most happy fate.
Whylst we in linke of loyall love thus led our restles life:
And whylst my careles hart did joye the chaunge of wonted strife.
I know not I, what cruell fact inforst my hartes delight:
My frend, myne own Ariodant, to worke this cruell spight.
On me, amidst the choking streames (oh fierse untimely death)
He drownd himself, & to the waves he did resigne his breath.
Whose death (oh hart) shal work thi wo and ende thy wonted joye:
And force my heavy head to learne, howe life I may destroy.
Yet know (oh Syr) in all this love, nought did offend but thought:
Nought trespased, but that unknown to thee (oh King) I sought   [K1^v]
To choose a feare of race unfit, unto your Princely state:
Whose royal tipe commaunds me choose a farre more fitter mate.
But if this gayne, by breach of lawe the death of scorching fyre:
Then do pronounce the sentence stayd tis death I so desire.
Only let this perswade your mynde no eye did ever see:
This corpse of myne, with whordoms blotte, so spotted for to bee.
This long discourse of amours past, and eke deniall made:
That never cloud of shame could yet her honor justly shade.
She stayd her wery jawes, and ends her heavy panting breath:
And wonted woes doo force her fall, in sound downe to the earth.
The aged King that sees this fitte, nye caught with like disease,
With shaking hands her temples rubs and seekes eche way tappease.

These choking griefs, but all in vain he rubs and chafes his childe:
For death hath nummed every part, and life is now exilde.
Til panting hart with strained might receives his wonted force:
And lets in wholsome breath againe into the senceles corse.   [K2^r]
Which joyful king (with hart revyvd) doth see and driveth feare
Away, and strayning then his sprites, he thus the Princes doth cheare.
I was or this resolved long of thy unspotted grace
My sweete and deare Jenevora, wherfore in hart displace.
These cankerd cares from tender brest feare not the paynes of death:
Let not the losse of desprate freend force thee resigne thy breath.
For I not only will provide for savegard of thy life:
But for a frend that shall thee please and gard thy hart from strife.
And kissing long her rubie lippes and wiping cleane her eyes:
He takes her by the christall hand and ceaseth to devise
Of former talke, and then himself, conveies her to her court:
Wher, (he once gone) she doth renew her wonted carefull sport.
But pensive king doth tract no tyme ne lenger makes delay:
For to provide a champion, to helpe in this assay.
Wherfore w^t blast of trompets sound it is proclaymed eche where:
That who so list in mortall fight his speare and armour beare.   [K2^v]
Against the stout Lurcanio, and conquere him in fight:
Shall have to wife Jenevora, and all her Princely right.
Now with this message prick ye postes the Herhautes trie their steades:
He rides to Brutus worthy realme, he takes the way that leades
To famouse Fraunce, & he doth hie unto an other soyle:
In fine, eche one for Princes doth by land and sea turmoyle.
But bootles do the Postes proclayme this booty daungerous:
For none list venter, for the gayne a deed so perilous.
Wherfore complet with cares they doo returne to court agayne:
And ther declare the ill successe, of this their message vayne.
But see the hap, one of these Postes returning voyd of ayde:
Rydes by the Hermitage, wheras Ariodant [hath] stayd.
And meeting then the Hermit ould, that sought for rootes abroade:
(Their greetings don) his hed he doth of message then unloade.
And showes unto the holy syre, howe Prince Jenevora
For lacke of ayde should burned be upon the second day.   [K3^r]
Ensuing next, and then he telles how she was first accusde
By one, that sayde by whordom vyle she had her selfe abusde.
Thus when they chatted had inough the Poste leaves of his talke:
And plies to court, and Hermit he unto his home doth walke.
Wher he no sooner is arivde, but (like to wonted sort)
These novels to his holy mate he doth forthwith report.
But who had seene ye countnaunce then of this Ariodant:
And markt how colour went & came and how his vaines did pant.

Mought wel have demde some present pange had vext his troubled
    minde :
And that by this report, his hart some straunge conceit did finde.
For troth, this tale no sooner toulde, and hard with open eare :
But swarming thoghts, in ravisht hed doo cluster now a reare.
Yet vertue, jelously doth blame. his fickell wavring minde :
And constancie condems his thoughts that flie like dust in wynde.
But amours old, provokes his harte to die in her defence :
Record of former amitie, forgettes supposd offence.   [K3ᵛ]
The diyng sparks of Cupides coales do now revive againe :
Her beutie great and comelines inforseth former payne.
His youthfull yeares begin to scorne such pinching miserie :
This pining diet makes him loth such holy penurie.
Hope doth assure him to winne her true and faithfull love :
If for her sake, in her defence : he will this battell prove.
Now nature, doth forbid him fight against Lurcanio :
(For he it is he knows right well) that was the Princes fo.
Love telles him that his brother hath deserved death by right :
In that he hath accused her that is the lampe of light.
Thus fansies rule within his head, as motions move the minde :
And changing thoughts do alter still, as reason right doth finde.
But to conclude devotion droups, poore penury is past :
Youth likes not now to purchase heven with faint and feeble tast.
The civill fight with brother, he regardes no whit at all :
His joye, his care, his life, his death, he cares not what befall.   [K4ʳ]
Wherfore, as he unknowen did come unto the Hermitage :
So he departs by stealth, without farewell to father age.
And wanders in the fieldes, till that the mantell blacke did hide :
The gladsome day and then he hyes unto the towne unspide.
Wher secretly he comes unto, his well approved host :
(Whose frendship stood him in great steed when cares annoyd him
    most.)
To whom when long he had discourst of his adventures all :
He doth disclose what he intends and sayes, (what so befall)
He will against his brother fight to save his Ladies life :
Or els before her, end his dayes, on point of brothers knife.
Wherfore, he willes him to provide, a complet armour sure :
That he the better may, against his brothers force indure.
And sturdy speare, & shield as stiffe he willes him to provide :
And barbed steed, both strong & light, that tempest like will glyde.
All these he willes him to prepare and all of colour black :
For Sables shall bewray (quoth he) of wanted joyes my wrack.   [K4ᵛ]
Thus leave I now the busy hoste, and eke coragious gest :
Preparing armour such as may defend the straunger best.

And to the court complet with care My pen and I must plie :
To tel their dole, their grief, their wo and mones of miserie.
The wery Postes are nowe returnd unto the heavy court :
Wher every one his sevrall hap doth dolefully report.
But when the aged king perceives, no ayde is to be found :
His weake and feeble limmes do fall for sorow to the ground.
His counsell eke (that see the cares of their unhappy king)
Doo feele welnie his griefe and smart and weepe, and wayle, and wring
Their fingers, & with drowned eyes lament his wretched state :
And with a thousand doles & plaints they rew his ruthfull fate.
Yet seyng him so sunke in grief, and fearing present death :
They seeke to banish diyng panges, by reasons wholesome breath.
But sooner mought ye mountain move or sea forsake his tide :
Then gnawing fits to want the force that through eche part do
    slide.   [K5^r]
Of wythard age, and crooked lymmes, and styng so feble hart :
That joye is gone, and blisse resingde, care turnes good happe to smart.
This is the sely Syers state, the Ladies leade like life :
With whome, nought els but teares, & cries, and heavines is ryfe.
For when they heare no helpe is founde, to ayde the Lady deare :
Eche chamber sounds of solom tunes, and cares bring dreadfull feare,
So much, that see in clustring heapes, whylst trembling maydens keepe,
And there, whylst with one perfect voyce, they wayle, they wo, and
    weepe :
This fearful soule, doth see (she thinkes) the shape of ougly sprightes :
She heares in rynging eare the sounde of clamors loud and skrykes.
The outmost of the prease, doth feale a pullyng hand to straine
Her slender arme, and shrinkes away, and couldly sweates for payne.
Thus feare, thus care, lamenting long, and spring of brackish teares :
With drouping dreade, and freating fittes, in hart opprest appeares,
But she, for whome was all this care, that had most cause to wayle,
Is voyde of carefulnes for death, ne griefe doth her assayle :   [K5^v]
Save death of her Ariodant, that was, then corsies bayne
More worse : wherfore for present deth she wisheth still in vaine.
Yet beares she with advised mynde, the Prelates sage advise :
That wils her to forget the world, and wonted joyes despise.
And biddes her call to mind, the blisse that never shall have ende :
Wherto by faith and stedfast troth she shortly shal assend.
He byddes her cast the feare of death, from bounds of godly brest :
For he can sheelde her hart (he saies) from payne, that bringeth rest.
He voucheth sacred scriptures now, to stablish her beliefe :
He tels what joy the soule receives, when flesh doth suffer griefe
And lastly, he perswades her that she gaines by giltles death,
A seate amongst the martyrd saints, that feede on heavenly breath.

As Abell doth, whose cruell death the cursed Cayn doth rewe,
Who movd with indignation, his native brother slew.
With these devout perswasions the Prince is mortifide,
Who doth for latest brunt of death with willyng minde abide.   [K6ʳ]
Amongst these passions tragicall and actes of endles care:
List now my Lordes, how Polinesse that wretched Duke doth fare.
Whose giltie mind findes littel ease, so much doth feare oppresse
His traitrous hart, least that Dalind his treason should confesse
Wherfore, (for greater suertie of this conceald offence)
He doth devise a cruell crime through mariage clokte pretence.
That is for to perswade Dalind the morow next, he will
By sacred law of spousals rightes, his promyse vowde fulfill.
And her consent once gotten, he deviseth for to send:
Her with two trusty men of his unto a wood, to thende.
There to bereve from her, her life insteede of wedlockes band:
Therby to ease his doughtfull breast that fearfull yet doth stand.
But whilst hereof his wits doo muse see wher Dalinda cummes:
Whose hasty pase and heavy cheare his sences throughly nummes.
To whom, her reverence performde, she shows how that the king
Hath geven unto the Steward charge that he foorthwith should
      bring.   [K6ᵛ]
Unto his presence, all the trayne of carefull Princes grace:
Of purpose to examine them of this accused case.
(I thinke qd she) wherfore my Lord, I thought convenient:
Upon a matter of such wayght, to know your wise intent.
This said, the subtil Duke (as though he weare to seeke for wittes)
A while with fixed eyes on ground on seate he musing sittes.
But when he had dissembled long his answere ready made:
With smiling cheer, & foulded armes thus unto her he sayd.
I never was deceivd (qd he) of thy assured troth
Mine own, and chiefest faithful frend to whom I would be loth
That any [jot] of foule mishappe, should chaunce or els befall:
Or that to any fretting grief, thy free mynde should be thrall.
But doo not thou dismay thy self I will provide for thee:
I will devise and seeke forthwith for thy best suertie.
I have a house not farre from hence, beyond the mightie wood:
Wherto I will thou do repayre, (if so thou thinkest good.)   [K7ʳ]
By breake of daye the morow next, where thou shalt stay for me,
Who wil upon the Princesse death, with speede come visit thee.
And ther by deede performe the thing that vow did earst protest,
By knitting thee the wedlocks knot that I so much request.
The doting mayde misdoughts no guyle she soone doth condiscende
Unto his tale, and all that night she doth in secrete spende.
But she once gon, the Duke sends for two trustie men of his,

Whose cursed hands with murdred bloud had ben imbrude ere this:
To whom when long he had discourst, what faith they ought to beare
Unto theyr Lord, and eke what troth within them ought tappeare:
He tels what forst him send for them and how it was his wyll:
That whylst they roade amydst the wood, they should Dalinda kyll
The ruffyns vile, with smal request movde to so foule a deede:
Consent unto their cruell Lord, and show them selves agreede
Unto his hest. Who for to move them more unto this sinne,
With promise great of large rewards he doth them fully winne.   [K7ᵛ]
By this the pensive daye is past, and now the mourning shade
Of black and fearefull night appeares: and doth eche where invade.
Wherin judge you what ease they take, that are wrapt in with wo,
And coucht in cave of carefulnes, and bathd in bed also:
Judge you the fathers quiet ease, and deeme the daughters rest,
Thinke how the goulden sleape doth please the ghost with griefe opprest.
And I will tell how night is gone, with countenance darke and sad:
Because amydst the restles court so littel ease he had.
And he thus gone Aurora showes her chearful visage gray,
And after her the blushing Phebe his countnance doth bewray.
Who scarce doth clime on lowest steppe, when as the watching mayde,
(Dalinda) leaves her lothed sleepe, and hasteth (as afrayde
To come to late) to Polinesse, who puttes her in the guide
Of those ungracious Ruffians, that he appoynts to ryde
With her, unto his house exprest, and biddes them tary there
(Dissemblyng wise) till he doth come to quench the sparkes of
    feare.   [K8ʳ]
(If any then did kindell in the rechles maydens minde)
Who hopes for troth, as erst she hard so every thing to finde.
Thus ryde they foorth, and riding I will leave them for a whyle:
And to the carefull court agayne that doth forthwith exile.
His drousie domps, I will returne and guyde my wery hand:
And of their last extreamest fittes who list to understand.
                                            shall heare the ende.
THe wery night hath brought again the dry and dreadfull day:
When heavy lookes, & cloudy sighes, a storme of cares bewray.
The court hath left his tossed couch, their restles bedde all shunne:
The ladies have their persing plaints and dolefull tune begonne.
Amidst a world of griefes the king forsakes his bathed bedde:
Who for the Prince Jenevora, a floud of teares hath shedde.
But kingly justice ruling still within his regall mind:
Doth tell him that the day is come which he of late assignde.
When either force of victors hand, should fade Lurcanio:
Or els in flames Jenevora, her sences should forgo.   [K8ᵛ]
These thoughts of justice force him cloke the anguish of his hart:

Affection lurkes in panting breast, in secreat lodgeth smart.
Wherfore in hastie wise he doth commaund unto the fyre
The giltles Princes whose desertes, gayne not so foule a byre.
Whose sentence known, Jenevora obeyes with pleased minde
Who decking her like her estate with jemmes of precious kinde.
Like hevenly ghost not earthly wight she teares her chariot straight
That coverd is with black, on whom a rought of Ladies waight.
Whose moorning weeds declare yᵉ cares of their disquiet hartes:
And argue to the gasing eye, the proufe of present smartes.
Next them, the king his train is past, whose heavy pensive cheare:
Agree with those black solom [sutes], which they that day did weare.
Then folows carefull Counselers, and then the aged king
In colour like, and after them a world of folke do fling.
In this aray, they are aryvde upon the dreadfull place:
Wher Princesse must resigne her lyfe, if that some sparke of grace. [L1ʳ]
Betyde her not, ther she abydes to tast her latest care:
Amidst the ghostly Prelates that of heavenly joyes declare.
The kyng scarce set on stately seate but all in complet steele
Lurcanio comes unto the liste, his chalenge to fulfill.
Who seene by false Duke Polinesse, that then was Martiall:
To guyde the feeld, he doth demaund of him the summe and all.
Of that he sought within the listes, to whom Lurcanio:
Thus sayd, I am approched here to prove against my fo.
That by the filthy whordoms crime, which I (qd he) did see:
Jenevora deserved hath, here burned for to bee.
This sayd, he entres in the lystes and by the relickes there:
In proufe of that which earst he said he doth devoutly sweare.
Nought wants but execution now, for that they only stay:
Which to performe, Jenevora concludes without delay.
Who first disrobes her selfe of all her Princely brave attire:
And only in her kyrtell she, doth mynde to taste the fire.   [L1ᵛ]
Then prostrate on the ground she falles, and with a cherefull voyce:
She prayes to God, with whom she hopes shortly for to rejoyce.
But who had seene the waylings then, of all the lookers on:
And how ech eye is drowned wᵗ tears and every mouth doth mone.
Mought wel have seen yᵉ mothers grief for death of loved childe:
And fathers plaint for native sonne, whose life feares death exilde.
Whilst thus the [Prince] prepares her selfe unto her heavy feast:
And whilst ech on lamenting stayes, with ruthfull sighyng breast.
See wher a Knight stands hovering, clad all in armour blacke:
And mounted on a barbed steede with sheeld behind his backe.
A mighty speare in hand he helde and swoord gyrt by his side,
His visar close before his face, least that he weare discride.
The Marshall spyes this Knight unknown: and as he sayd before,

So now he doth demaund also, of him, the cause, wherfore:
He is arivd in that aray amydst that worthy presse,
To whom Ariodant doth these knightlike wordes expresse:　　　[L2ʳ]
To save (qd he) from fyry flames this false accused wight:
Though Scots do feare, I do intend, to venter life and might:
Nought doughting but as giltles she condempned is to die:
So this my spear and sword (I trust) her truth right well shall trie.
The straunger enters thus the listes wher stoutly he doth sweare:
That of that fowle supposed crime Jenevora is cleare.
This don, without a lenger stay, the Heraultes crie to fight:
Now do your best, & god him sheeld that drawes his sword in right.
Lurcanio leaves now to muse, his speare is coucht in rest:
He forward like the winde doth fling with sheld before his brest:
Ariodant, not ignorant with whom he is to fight:
Sets forward to with thundring pase and meetes his brother right.
The spears all crusht do mount aloft eche keepes his saddell sure:
Ariodant against his fo, doth mightely indure.
Then leave they foming steades, & then they draw their shining blades:
Wherwith ech one his enemy, with courage stout invades.　　　[L2ᵛ]
He smytes a carving blowe upon, his adversaries shelde:
And he doth send a cantell from, his helmet to the feelde.
Lurcanio is nothing nice, of his approved might:
Ne yet Ariodant behinde, his almes for to requight.
But farre unegall is the match, Lurcanio seemes to play:
When as Ariodant is forst, to ward, or els decay.
Yet as he can he lendes a blowe, and then he shiftes againe:
From dint of brothers stroke, whose forse would well requite his payne.
Thus he doth strike, and he the blow receives upon his shelde:
And he againe, (the vantage spyde) a buffet byg doth yelde.
Lurcanio thinks of brothers death, and fightes like Lyon fierse:
Ariodant, (his Ladie spied) both steele and male doth pearse,
With bluddy blads thei prick & thrust the ground is dyde with bloude
Now breath they both, & now againe they rage like Tigers wood
In this conflict I must them leave, eche seeking others ende:
And to Dalinda once againe, my pen and I must bende.　　　[L3ʳ]
Who once aryvde within the wood, wher she must yeld her life:
In steed of solom mariage, on edge of Ruffyns knyfe.
They bid her light of from her horse, and with a countnance fiers:
The sum of that they had in charge to her they do rehears.
Which when she knew, from wonted talk her closed lippes refrayne:
And feare of death do force her feele the panges of deadly payne.
Her careles head, late occupide with blissed wedlockes bandes
Is comefortles, & now poore wretch as stone in wall she standes.
So farre her present thoughts be od, as hope of suertie:

And now to sure signes of smart and stormes of miserie.
But making of necessitie a present vertue, she
Decrees as time did serve to make her soule from bondage free.
And kneling then upon the ground betwixt these ghostly mates:
That mynd by carving of her head to ende her latest fates.
She prayes unto the Creator to pardon her offence:
And that he would forget her sinne and way her penitence. [L3ᵛ]
Then wᵗ a streame of tears she rews her Ladies giltles death:
For whom, the anguish of her hart, doth choke welny her breath.
What should I say, for thousand sins which she did never know:
(To length yᵉ time) she praies to God that he will mercy show.
But see how in most daungerous tydes oft times doth happen blisse:
See how in present stroke of death the hart releeved is.
Whilst thus she prays adventure drove through search of nearest way:
To Scottish court, upon the place wher she devout doth pray.
The famous knight Raynaldo, who beholding with his eye:
Betwixt two Ruffians naked swords a Lady prest to die.
He spurs his Steed, & draws his blade and drives unto them twoo:
In mynde to [rescue] if he could that carefull wight from woo.
The tormenters that saw him come dispayring of their might:
Forsake yᵉ mayd & mount on Steeds and save them selves by [flight].
Which when Dalinda vews, she thus unto Raynald gan say:
Yet let me crave this curtesie or thou depart away. [L4ʳ]
(Oh worthy Knight,) that is, yᵗ thou wilt be my guyde unto
The most unhapiest Scottish court and most complete with woe.
Wher I shal bring the joyfulst news that ever came to kyng:
And tell the gladdest tale that earst, a messenger did bring.
Raynaldo grauntes to her desire she is now horst againe:
They forward poste, and as they ride she greatly doth complaine.
Of false Duke Polinessos guyle she blames his subtill witte:
And for revenge to god she cries for such offence most fitte.
Thus weary time is spent, and now they are within the vewe:
Of flaming bronds of glistring swords and of the Scottish crewe.
Then with a strayned halowing voice stay how Raynaldo cries:
Depart the Knightes, & with yᵗ word eene casteth up his eyes.
To see from whence proceeds yᵉ voice that ringes so in their eares:
And therwithall Raynaldo and Dalinda, do appeare.
Who passing throgh yᵉ mightie prease, at last approche the seate:
Of Scottish King, wheras Dalind beginnes for to intreate. [L4ᵛ]
Of all the treason which the Duke and she did late devise,
But crying first, staye Polinesse, thus to her tale she plies.
Why shuld I lenger stay (oh wretch) why should my lippes refrayn
From sounding out the perfect troth which hidden, seekes to stayne
The giltles Imphe of vertues schoole whose spotlesse troth doth crie

For just revenge for such offence, to him that rules skie.
Oh king let dought of daughters crime, no more dismaye thy mynde,
Ne let thy hart to feareful thoughts, for princes be inclinde:
For this thryse cursed tongue of myne, shall plainly show to thee:
Who did offende, who gaind this fire, from which the prince is free.
And though mine own reproch, I must blase here amidst this presse,
Yet gnawing thoughts of gilty minde, inforce me troth confesse.
This Duke (oh king) this Polinesse this false disceitful Knight
And I unhappiest wretch it was, that gaynd these flames of right,
For see disceit: whilst in the court, I led a rechles race,
And whylst amongst the courtly trayne, I servde the princes grace. [L5ʳ]
There came to me this Polinesse, who with a smyling chere,
And glosing woords gan long discourse what friendship he did beare
To me, and how his whole desire was to obteyne my love
Which for to get with tedious sute, he seekes me long to prove.
But see, as forced watch doth make, the savage Hauke to fist:
As strained bitte the Coult untamd, doth make apt to the list:
So did this Dukes continuall sute enforce me to consent:
In hope of lawfull mariage, unto his false intent.
The conquest gaind, he showes him pleas'd, and I, in hope of blisse,
Doo finde my selfe not discontent, at thappy happe of this.
This past, and I remayning still within the princesse court:
Upon a day Duke Polinesse thus to me gan report.
If that I thought my former woords wherof such perfect force,
As mought (qd he) from wavering minde all damps of dought devorce:
I would refraine that now I mynde in presence here declare,
And closly in my secrete mynde, such passions I would spare.   [L5ᵛ]
But deede shal showe the summe (qd he,) of my well meaning hart,
And eke in woordes my just intent, to thee I shall impart.
Thou knowst (qd he) what goulden tyme in service I have spent:
In hope to gayne at last for hyre the princesse like assent.
Thou partli knowst, my faithful hart and loyall love to hir:
Thou knowest what divers waies I us'd hir friendship for to styre.
But only I to wel have known how evel she did requite
My vowed troth, and how my love, she had in great despite.
Which when with griefe I vewd (qd he) I sought by reasons skill
To maister love, and by advise to tame affections will.
And thinking that the second nayle, could soone expell the first,
I hardly finde this moysture can asswage my former thrust.
Thus tost am I with bylowes great of great unrest (qd he)
And onely finde by sage advise, this only suertie.
I thinke (qd he) the heavens it will, that that selfe same attyre
Which she did weare, when first I did so much her love desire.   [L6ʳ]
Should quite my former thraled hart, of evell requited love:

And from thy breast if doughts remayne dispairing doughts remove.
Wherfore I will, that with those robes, that prince in feast doth weare
Hard by the outwast houses thou Dalinda shalt appeare
To me where I in scorne of prince will tosse her princely trayne:
And ther resigne the latest fittes, of my long proved payne.
With smal request I graunted have to his so sugred tale:
And to thappointed place also, to come I did not fayle.
Wher I in robes princes grace, when sleape the prince possest:
With Juels, tablets, cheins, & ringes, did yelde to his request.
This same was it, and that was I whome straunger so did see:
The night when feast in court was helde wherof princesse is free.
But heare oh king the ende of all, judge of this traitrous part,
See how the filed woords agreed, with false disceitfull hart.
When giltles thus Lurcanio had accus'd the princesse grace
And when for trial of her truth the tyme and setted place.   [L6ᵛ]
Was known to all, Duke Polinesse still caught I thinke with feare
Least that this treason done by us mought any wayes appeare:
And doughting still my secret mynde he sought the only way
By former pleasant fained woords, to worke my last decaye.
And feeding then my hungry vayne, with Duches princely state:
He mindes to put in practise now, his long pretensed hate.
And sending me with Ruffians two, unto a desert woode:
(In steede of present mariage,) he seekes to shead my bloud.
But see, betwixt their dredful blades whylst knelyng I dyd pray,
And whilst for ende of my last words the tormenters did staye:
This Knight, my guide, aryvd upon, the place where I should dye:
Who savd my lyfe and forst my fooes, to leave theyr armes, and flye,
Thus have you hard oh king (qd she) the troth of treason strong,
My gained death, his like desert, and your sustayned wrong.
The summe of all this cruel crime, disclos'd thus to eche eare:
Revives theyr dying cares that earst were caught with dreadfull
    feare.   [L7ʳ]
But Polinesse that heares theffect of all this cruell deede
Disclosed thus, a heape of griefes which in his head doo breede.
Yet as he had a countnance earst to woorke his owne decaye:
So he denies all that which now Dalinda did bewray:
And proferst ther upon to trie, his troth against his foe
In combat fight, and gauntlet he, unto the ground doth throw
As chalenger, which Raynold spies, and doth receive his gage,
In mynde without a lenger stay the battell for to wage.
And once arayde in every point, fit for a mortall fight:
They mount on Steeds, and with the speares eche seekes his foe to spight.
Duke Polinesse discharged hath, his speare that clymes the skies:
But through both breast and backe the speare of stout Raynaldo hies.

Which when the Duke perceives, and feeles, the panges of present death:
And knowes his life doth fade away through want of gasping breath:
He yeldes him selfe as recreant, and dying doth confesse,
In circumstance, the treason which Dalinda did expresse.   [L7ᵛ]
And how inforst throgh jelous minde which he did then suspect,
Twixt princesse and Ariodant, he was therto direct.
Then how his last devise he usde to move Ariodant:
That only his desired love the Prince in hart did plant.
Which only sight I know (qd he) was cause of straungers death
And with that woord his sinful soule resingde his wicked breath.
Whose carcase was no sooner dead, and life had lost his force:
But in the mydst of flashing flames, his wounded senceles corse
Entombed was, with joyful shouts, that God did save the right,
And with deserved punishment, he did the giltie quight.
But she, whose fixed mynde to die, did loth a lenger lyfe:
Augmenteth rather wonted woes then wants hir former strife.
Wherfore she is in mynde oftymes to taste the force of fyre,
For rather that, then lothsome lyfe, she gladly gan requyre.
The king whose aged head did earst tast never such great joye
To see the princesse giltles tryde, doth wonted cares distroy.   [L8ʳ]
Who first calles for Ariodant that fought for Princes grace:
Of whom he frendly craves the sight of his desired face.
Wherfore his head peece layde aside, his visage is bewrayde:
And then to pensive Princes thus, he kneelyng briefly sayd,
How nere oh thrise renouned prince had falshood brought to ende
Thy woorthy race, whose spotles lyfe with saynts may wel contend?
How nere had tresons force prevaild how neare had vile disceit
Entrald thy noble giltles hart, with hidden falshods baytes?
But oh how neare had my mistrust, ben cause of thy decaye:
Whose wretched head to sugred talke to greatly did obey?
Wherfore not only Polinesse, ne this Dalind deserve,
A shamefull death, but myser I, whose faithles hart did swerve
So farre from duties lore, as gaines an everlasting paine:
And as he would have ferder sayd, (through griefe) his lippes refrayn
From farder talke, and sences fayle, and he doth fall to ground:
And ther he lies, berevd of breath, and chokt with fainting sounde. [L8ᵛ]
But when Jenevora had vewde long tyme with persing eye:
The face of her Ariodant: and plainly eke gan spye.
By countnance, loke, by shape, & speach the same her freend to bee:
Whom greedy stream had forst she feard to die in misery.
Oh judges that can, what fansies then did rule within her mynd:
What passing joy, what happy blisse her crased brayne did finde.
For neither head, ne tongue, ne hand can think, can tell, or wryte:
The least or smalest percell of her late conceyvde delight.

Not she her selfe, can ease the toyle of joyfull panting hart:
Whose striving force extreme delight to traunce doth straight convert.
And there as in a quiet sleape, a whyle she doth remayne:
But once revyvde, her dryry lippes, she thus to speake did strayne.
And doth the guyder of my life, the only proppe and stay:
Of this my wery limmes, yet lyve? oh happy thryse I say.
Oh blessed fates, and dost thou live? and do these eyes behould:
Thy wished shape, whose comly lims these armes so oft have fould. [M1ʳ]
And lives in deed Ariodant, Jenevoras delight:
And was it he that for his frend, so manfully did fight?
Oh soppe of joye more pleasant farre then wealth of worldly blisse:
Oh soveraigne salve, nought cures so well the crased hart as this.
Oh welcome thou more deare to me, then goods, then frendes, then life:
A gest more gladder to my hart then cares earst caused strife.
Thy health doth force me wish yᵗ life which fame of thy decay
Intised late through heavy lot, to scrine in cloddes of clay.
Amidst this tale a thousand tymes, they frendly do imbrace:
And with their silver trickling drops eche bathe others face.
She layes her happy head upon her joyfull lovers brest:
And he agayne his body bendes: to yeld his Lady rest.
Thus now in words, & now in deedes and now by signes of love:
Ech shows, yᵗ joyned faithfull hartes doth such affections move.
The sight wherof brings youth again unto the aged King:
Whose trembling hart, for very joye in blissfull breast doth
   spring.   [M1ᵛ]
But when this great felicitie, had vanquisht every care:
And when amidst this world of joye, eche on receivde his share.
Then by commaundement trompets sound and oyes loude is cride,
Wherfore the rought give audience, and then the king thus sayd:
How farre we are indetted to the heavenly powers devine:
My lords & frends, you have wel seen this day before your eyne.
As both by fatall chaunce, how this vyle treason was bewrayd:
As how by knightly prowesse, which Ariodant assayde.
Against his native brother, he hath savde Jenevora:
From fyry flames, & brought us health that lookt for last decay.
And last, how falshod payed is with death for gaind desert:
A myrror good, for such as live, infect with traytors hart.
Wherfore as bounden dutie biddes, first let us yelde the prayse:
To him, that quites the innocent, and payes the false alwayes.
And we (as reasons lore doth charge) will seeke for to requite:
Forthwith received benefittes, with all our power and might.   [M2ʳ]
For as to thou Ariodant, for this thy noble hart:
Thy curtesie, and loyall love, we yelde thee this as part.
Of recompence, take thou to wife the Prince Jenevora,

And we, for maintnaunce of your states will soone provyde a stay.
Be thou to her a faithfull feare, and she a loving wyfe :
Beare dutie to thy Lord and King, whilst thou hast breath and life.
And sith by thee syr knight unknown, this treason came to light :
We will as best shal please thy hart thy frendship well requite.
Lurcanio eke, sith brothers death provokt thee to this ire :
Shalt freely live, and use our grace, as thou shalt best desire.
For pardon of Jenevora, small sute I think will serve :
Whose gentil mynd from pities lore as yet did never swarve.
But as to thee Dalinda, sith thou soughtst by treason vyle :
To seeke thy mistres death, we will that thou into exile.
For ever shalt be put, and eke to runne a banisht race,
Till better hope of truer hart, shall winne thee favours grace.   [M2ᵛ]
This sentence sayde, the tossed caps doo cutte the cloudie skie :
And everi mouth, with strained voice God save the King doo crie.
The lovers two, on ground prostrate a thousand thankes impart.
Unto theyr Liege and Soveraigne, with most contented hart.
But to recount what passions past, betwixt the brothers twayne,
Would make an other history, and woorke my treble payne.
Wherfore let this suffise, my Lordes, not one but lyves in joye,
Not one there is amidst the prease, that cares doo now annoy.
Amidst which myrth, to court again the King and all returne :
And as they ryde, in signe of joye, eche doth the streates adorne :
With tynsell bright, with arras riche and glistring cloth of goulde :
And ladies pearch on wyndowes hie the lovers to behould
Who passe the streates with happy harts, and so arive on court.
Wher every one seekes to augment, his late received sport.
And wher, upon a solome daye, appointed by the king,
The Princesse and Ariodant, with sacred woords and Ring :   [M3ʳ]
Receyve the ryght of mariage, as gladde to them as lyfe :
Who long in blisse did spend their daies and died devoyde of stryfe.

FINIS.

NOTES to *The Historie*

The black letter of the original has been altered to roman, but no change has been made in spelling or punctuation except as noted below. Certain letters have been altered: long "s" is printed as modern "s," "u" and "v" are distinguished according to modern usage as are consonant and vowel "i," while "vv" is printed as "w." Abbreviations involving the omission of a nasal consonant have been silently lengthened. Although no capitals have been altered to lower case, several lower case letters printed as the first letter of the initial word of a line have been silently altered to capitals. In the original the lineation divides each seven-foot line into two lines: a four-foot and a three-foot line.

Editorial comment has been restricted to those words or phrases which affect the reading and those whose meanings are not readily ascertained by reference to the *O.E.D.*

A7^v, l. 4. chase: case, O. Both here and in A8^r, l. 11 the meaning requires "chase."

A8^v, l. 11. chase: case, O.

B2^v, l. 5. lippes: libbes, O. The spelling is possible but it is not used elsewhere in the text.

B3^v, l. 5. unegall: venegall, O.

B5^v, l. 2. eare: tare, O.

B7^v, l. 12. vanes: vaue, O. I take the original to be "vane" with a turned letter on the assumption that "fanes"—pieces of colored cloth—is the word intended with the alternate "v" in place of "f."

B8^v, l. 7. gods: goods, O.

C2^v, l. 7. cold, O. The meaning, "hidden," is clear both here and in l. 4 of C4^v. It may be that this is a past participle of "coll" but that verb is usually applied to people, not things.

C6^v, l. 2. had: hah, O.

C7^v, l. 11. requite: require, O.

C8^v, l. 6. Sopors: Sopros, O.

D2^r, l. 11. graunte: graune, O.

D2^v, l. 13. tould: could, O.

D7^v, l. 9. course: crurse, O.

D7^v, l. 10. glayve: glayne, O.

D8^r, l. 10.): omitted in O.

E1^r, l. 6. write: wpite, O.

E1^r, l. 12. live: line, O.

E2^r, l. 5. oft: of, O.

E7^r, l. 1. forsed, O. The *O.E.D.* gives the meaning of "like" or "fancy" for this; compare "forcing" on C2^r, l. 12.

E7^v, l. 15. thy: the, O.

E8^r, l. 12. these: thse, O.

F2^v, l. 14. indetted: indected, O. Compositor used the wrong ligature. Elsewhere the "tt" ligature is used for this word.

F4^v, l. 3. in best: in his best, O.

F6^v, l. 8. deare, O. Daze, paralyze, or render helpless.

F6^v, l. 15. (: omitted in O.

F7^v, l. 7. knows: know, O. The final "s" probably omitted by compositor because with "w" he reached the right margin.

F7^v, l. 9. crased fort, O. Broken fort; cf. "batterd castell," F7^r, l. 12.

G1^r, l. 12. A: As, O.

G2^v, l. 16. ought: oughe, O.

G5^v, l. 5. Creseids: Greseids, O.

G6^r, l. 1. (: omitted in O.

G8^v, l. 6. ywrought: I wrought, O.

H1^v, l. 4. he: I, O.

H3^r, l. 5. Is: In, O.

H3^v, l. 1. lure: sure, O.

H3^v, l. 5. force: forcy, O.

H3^v, l. 11. of: or, O.

H5^r, l. 13. setted: letted, O.

H5^v, l. 9. performe: forme, O.

H6^r, l. 12. foorth: sooth, O.

H7^r, l. 3. (: omitted in O.

H7^r, l. 13. sayd: The meaning "contaminated" is clear from the context, but I have been unable to find any other use of the word.

H8^v, l. 3. though: thought, O.

H8^v, l. 10. yelde: yelne, O.

I1^r, l. 12. plants, O. Variant of "plaints."

I4^r, l. 3. (: omitted in O.

K3^r, l. 12. hath: Not in O but here added to make the line metrically correct.

K7^r, l. 11. jot: yot, O. An unusual misuse of "y" for "i."

K8^v, l. 4. exile, O. The meaning is "exhale" but the rhyme requires the present spelling.

L1^r, l. 7. teares, O. This may be an aphetic form of "enters," analogous with "terment" for "interment."

L1^r, l. 12. sutes: lutes, O.

L2^r, l. 7. Prince: Princesse, O. Elsewhere Genevra is called Prince and metrically this form is here needed.

L4^r, l. 12. rescue: reseue, O.

L4^r, l. 14. flight: fight, O.

L6^r, l. 12. thrust, O. A variant spelling of "thirst." The pronunciation is indicated by the rhyme with "first." Cf. A8^v where "thrust" rhymes with "wurst."

M1^r, l. 5. iudges, O. This is the northern form of the imperative.

M1^r, l. 12. dryry, O. This is a variant form of "dreary," meaning "bloody."